UNDERSTANDING YOUR MORMON NEIGHBOR

UNDERSTANDING
YOUR
MORMON NEIGHBOR

A Quick Christian Guide for Relating to Latter-Day Saints

ROSS ANDERSON

ZONDERVAN.com/
AUTHORTRACKER
follow your favorite authors

ZONDERVAN

Understanding Your Mormon Neighbor
Copyright © 2011 by Ross Anderson

This title is also available as a Zondervan ebook.
Visit www.zondervan.com/ebooks.

Requests for information should be addressed to:

Zondervan, *Grand Rapids, Michigan 49530*

Library of Congress Cataloging-in-Publication Data

Anderson, Ross.
     Understanding your Mormon neighbor : a quick Christian guide for relating to the
    Latter-day Saints / Ross Anderson.
        p. cm.
    Includes bibliographical references
    ISBN 978-0-310-32926-8 (softcover)
    1. Church of Jesus Christ of Latter-day Saints — Doctrines. 2. Mormons. I. Title.
    BX8635.3.A53 2011
    22230'.9332 — dc22

2011006391

Cover design: Tammy Johnson
Interior design: Cindy LeBreacht

Printed in the United States of America

HB 02.22.2023

CONTENTS

PREFACE

WHEN IT COMES TO Mormonism, I am an insider and an outsider. I grew up in an active Latter-day Saint family and have lived among the Mormons in Utah for almost thirty years. Yet, I have not been a Mormon since early adulthood. As a young man, I rejected the teachings of Mormonism and subsequently embraced an evangelical version of the historic, biblical Christian faith. Though no longer part of the inner circle, I retain a respect for Mormonism's values and a certain cultural resonance with its people.

As Claudia Bushman notes in *Contemporary Mormonism*, insider views of the world of the Latter-day Saints (LDS) are suspected of lacking objectivity while outsider views often fail to penetrate and capture the life of Mormons in a way recognizable to those on the inside. Since my time on the inside, Mormonism has changed and I have forgotten much. My experience never included the temple ritual or a two-year mission. So in this book, I supplement my firsthand knowledge with research from other sources, from both insiders and outsiders. My stance as a former Mormon might lead some to assume that I am antagonistic. I am not. I strive to be as fair and accurate as I can from within my own perspective.

The aim of this study is not an in-depth examination of LDS beliefs. Rather, I hope to produce a description of Mormon life that is recognizable by both Latter-day Saints and intelligible to non-Mormon readers, free of the weaknesses common to both insider and outsider accounts.

My goal is threefold. First, I want to foster a congenial perspective. I hope the general reader will better understand the Mormon people in order to relate to them better as a growing force in American social and political life. For example, this book may help readers to understand the faith of political candidates like Mitt Romney and why Latter-day Saints rally so strongly for certain social issues, as they did in the 2008 battle over California's Proposition 8.

Second, I want to stimulate my fellow evangelicals to think new thoughts about how to engage Mormonism. Evangelicals tend to examine Mormonism merely in terms of its doctrinal beliefs, yet Christian missiology teaches us the importance of cultural analysis and contextualization. I will try to explain and model in these pages an approach that goes beyond cognitive debate to consider Mormons as whole persons in the context of their culture.

Third, I wish to encourage traditional Christians to enter relationships with Latter-day Saints in order to engage in spiritual conversations and faith-sharing. The LDS Church claims to offer traditional Christians an upgrade to their faith. My conviction is that biblical Christianity actually has a great deal to offer Latter-day Saints. Increasing numbers of Mormons find their faith narrative and cultural experience unsatisfying. As they consider other alternatives, I would like to equip evangelicals to share the historic Christian faith narrative as an option, and churches to better assist former Latter-day Saints as they navigate the cultural and theological journey from one faith family into another.

Every group has its own preferred terminology. While the Church of Jesus Christ of Latter-day Saints is commonly known as the Mormon Church, Latter-day Saints want to be called by the official title. This is cumbersome for the writer and the reader. As an alternative, I will refer to "the LDS Church" or simply "the Church" in most cases.

At times, I will use the terms "Mormon" and "LDS" as adjectives to refer to the Church and to elements of the culture that it creates. I will also use the terms "Mormon" and "Saint" as nouns to refer to the people themselves. All of this is in keeping with common practice observed even by LDS authors.

As a noted LDS anthropologist has written: "The finite limitations of memory and experience mean that no picture we develop can serve for long without challenge."[1] Despite the errors in this work that will surely arise from my limitations of memory, experience, and ability, I trust the picture I paint can serve the reader well for some time to come.

Ross Anderson
Roy, Utah
December 2010

1

MORMONISM: CULT OR CULTURE?

I N THE FIRST decade of the twenty-first century, the Church of Jesus Christ of Latter-day Saints and its members have emerged into the national spotlight. Media from around the world featured the LDS Church in stories about the 2002 Winter Olympics. In 2008, the Latter-day Saints played a prominent role in California's Proposition 8 vote over homosexual marriage. Church President Thomas S. Monson has been named the most influential eighty-year-old in America. Mitt Romney ran for President. Harry Reid became the Senate majority leader. David Archuleta and Ken Jennings won fame on TV shows *American Idol* and *Jeopardy*, respectively. Glenn Beck gained a national audience as a political commentator. Stephanie Meyer sold millions of vampire novels.[1] As the fourth largest denomination in the United States — and the richest per capita — the LDS Church has become a mainstream force,[2] despite making up only about 2 percent of the American adult population.[3]

Latter-day Saints don't just live in Utah anymore. By 1990 about 30 percent of U.S. Mormons lived outside the western states, due in part to increased mobility in America after World War II as well as ongoing missionary activity. Many Americans have encountered Mormonism through familiar images like missionaries on bicycles, the Mormon Tabernacle Choir, or the Mormons' tightly knit families and clean lives.[4] Almost half of all Americans actually know an active or devout Latter-day Saint. Most of us (71 percent) have seen Mormon ads on TV, and almost two-thirds of Americans have been approached by LDS missionaries at some time.[5]

The Mormon people are very much like other Americans. They are about average in a wide variety of family attitudes and behaviors, overall happiness, marital happiness, and self-esteem. They are somewhat better educated, a bit more politically conservative, and slightly more favorable to minority rights and civil rights than typical Americans.

MITT ROMNEY, CANDIDATE FOR PRESIDENT OF THE UNITED STATES. © Christopher Halloran. Shutterstock.com. Used by permission.

Yet, in other areas, Mormons are measurably different. They sacrifice significantly more than most Americans for their religious beliefs: they go to church more, give more, and serve more. They are more likely to be white. They have a lower mortality rate from cancer and cardiovascular disease. Of course, there are also major theological differences between Mormonism and the traditional forms of Christianity to which most Christians in America subscribe.

Some facets of Latter-day Saint life appear strange to outsiders. The private nature of temple worship, which is highly sacred to Mormons, conveys a secretive image. The public expresses some suspicion and fear about whether Latter-day Saints will use their organizational abilities, wealth, and political power to manipulate society for their religious goals.[6] Some people are antagonized by the exclusivist claims of the LDS Church, which claims to be the only church on earth with the authority to act or speak for God. Americans are also confused about the relationship of the LDS Church to its polygamous history and to contemporary splinter groups.

MORMONISM AS A CULTURE

To be Mormon is far more than being a member of a particular church. Mormonism is an all-encompassing way of life.[7] One prominent LDS scholar observes that "Mormons still think of themselves as a people as much as a church."[8] Like Islam, Mormonism is not merely a set of beliefs but a complete identity. To belong to the LDS community entails a deep commitment to the shared customs, values, and lifestyle of the Latter-day Saint culture.[9]

When I speak of "culture," I mean the particular ways of thinking, speaking, and living that are shared by people with a common past and identity.[10] People who live in the United States partake of a unique culture that is birthed from our common identity as Americans. Even within America, smaller religious and ethnic groups have subcultures that are distinct from the larger whole. We don't learn our culture consciously but absorb it simply by being around other members of our group. Based on common beliefs and worldview,[11] the Mormon culture — like any other — takes shape in patterns of language, in folklore, in organizational structures, in buildings and artifacts, in forms of art, in ritual and other shared experiences, and in expectations of how people will act.

Every culture expresses itself in unique vocabulary and language patterns. Mormons pray in a distinctive style, using common jargon and intonation. As John Sorenson notes, "Thousands of words, phrases, names and stylistic features have peculiar LDS significance,"[12] including common LDS euphemisms ("Oh my heck!"), words that describe LDS life ("ward" or "endowment"), and phrases that describe core features of the LDS worldview ("the pre-existence" or "second estate").

Every culture expresses itself in ritual. Latter-day Saint beliefs take shape through the words and actions of common rituals such as baptism, anointing the sick, priesthood ordination, the intricate rites of the temple ordinances,[13] and unique LDS death and burial customs.[14]

Mormon culture reflects a strong value of music, drama, and dance.[15] Mormonism's rich musical history includes the value of musical training in the home[16] and traditional forms of sacred music using piano, organ, and choirs.[17] The dominant form of drama in the LDS world is the pageant, like the Hill Cumorah Pageant, an outdoor spectacle that proclaims the themes of Mormon history and scripture in a tone of triumphant celebration.[18] A small LDS cinematic industry produces films that depict the great stories of Mormonism or poke fun at LDS cultural quirks. Social dancing has always been part of Mormon social life, following precedents set by its earliest leaders. Public dance festivals are also popular.[19]

Mormonism has a rich folklore. The most common folk stories reflect themes that Latter-day Saints find most important, like the pioneer past. Mormon folklore also encourages faithfulness by rooting the Saints in a cosmic struggle between good and evil.[20]

Latter-day Saints express their underlying values through physical objects and symbols, such as the image of the Salt Lake Temple, the beehive, and the angel Moroni.[21] They use art to illustrate historical events and religious stories central to their message. One of the most common themes in LDS art is the "First Vision" of Joseph Smith,

© Daniel Anderson. Used by permission.

which began his prophetic mission.[22] Mass-produced consumer objects, such as Book of Mormon action toys and Mormon-themed T-shirts, reinforce the Mormon cultural identity.[23]

As with any group, these various cultural expressions serve to identify insiders versus outsiders. One example is the popular CTR ring. CTR stands for "Choose the Right," a theme reinforced in the LDS children's program. Intended as a reminder to make good moral choices, CTR rings make Latter-day Saints instantly recognizable to each other, creating a bond of common identity.[24]

A number of Latter-day Saint customs have a similar role as cultural boundary markers.[25] The Word of Wisdom, which prohibits alcohol, coffee, and tobacco, identifies Mormons to outsiders and communicates one's standing inside the LDS community. Many Saints hang photographs of a temple, or of the current LDS Church President, on the walls of their homes. Even wearing apparel from Brigham Young University identifies people as part of the group.

SHAPING THE MORMON IDENTITY

The cultural identity of Latter-days Saints has been powerfully shaped by shared historical experiences. The trek of the Mormon pioneers to Utah in 1847 is central to the sense of Mormon "peoplehood." Stories of the pioneer journeys are recounted often to inspire pioneer-like virtues in contemporary Mormons.[26] The journey is interpreted by Latter-day Saints as parallel to the exodus of Israel in the Bible, confirming the Mormon claim of being restored Israel.[27] Pioneer Day is enthusiastically celebrated — especially in the West — with parades, rodeos, carnivals, and religious services that commemorate the day the Saints arrived in Utah.[28]

Pioneer virtues and skills are maintained in contemporary values and practices. Many LDS women still practice quilting, sewing, canning, and other crafts that connect them with the lives of their forebears — crafts that also reflect the self-reliant pioneer spirit that is alive and well in Mormonism today. Mormons help each other out during times of need as a way of fostering self-sufficiency and expressing self-reliance — just as their forebears did.

Another part of the historical legacy that shapes Mormon identity is persecution. The reason the Saints fled to Utah was, in part, to escape persecution. The persistent memory of wrongs committed against them wherever they settled can translate into a persecution complex. Latter-day Saints can bear the mantle of the persecuted minority quite readily, and they are often sensitive to criticism and intolerant of critics.[29]

People enter the LDS cultural community in two ways: by birth or by conversion. Converts become integrated into their new identity by first embracing the LDS message and then by assimilating into the lifestyle and cultural ethos of Mormonism.[30] Birthright Saints, by contrast, typically move through a succession of stages or events that reinforce their sense of belonging to a unique people.[31]

The first of these formative events is the blessing of infants. In the weekly Sunday gathering, the baby is brought before the congregation, encircled by priesthood holders, and given a name and a blessing;[32] this event marks the child's initial inclusion in the faith community.

LATTER-DAY SAINTS REENACT THEIR PIONEER PAST. © Melnee Benfield. Used by permission.

Most LDS children are then baptized at the age of eight, which is considered "the age of accountability." Children are baptized by total immersion, by someone holding the LDS priesthood (a family member if possible). Following baptism, the child receives "the gift of the Holy Ghost," bestowed by a priesthood holder placing his hands on the child's head and imparting a verbal blessing and prayer. The child is then confirmed as a formal member of the Church of Jesus Christ of Latter-day Saints. Adult converts to Mormonism go through baptism and confirmation in the same way, often being baptized by the missionary who converted them.[33]

For male children, the LDS identity is further reinforced by initiation into the priesthood. Latter-day Saints understand the priesthood as "the authority to act in the name of God."[34] The LDS priesthood has two levels. Aaronic Priesthood is available to worthy boys once they reach age twelve. At adulthood, young men typically advance to the Melchizedek Priesthood, which confers greater authority. Priesthood reinforces a man's position, roles, and responsibilities as part of the faith community.

During their later teen years, Mormon youth of both genders are encouraged to seek a patriarchal blessing. As a once-in-a-lifetime event, the patriarchal blessing is a personalized prophecy given in a private ceremony by a priesthood leader specially ordained for this role. Such blessings typically include general promises about future events, along with encouragement to live a worthy life. Patriarchal blessings are usually shared only with family members and are privately treasured and pondered for insights into life circumstances and future events.[35]

For young men and women, serving a proselytizing mission for the LDS Church socializes them into their LDS identity in a powerful way and prepares them for a lifetime of participation in the LDS community.[36] In preparation for a mission or as part of a temple marriage, Latter-day Saints are introduced into the ritual of the temple through a rite called the endowment (see chapter 6).

MISSIONARY SERVICE IS A COMMON RITE OF PASSAGE FOR YOUNG LDS MEN AND WOMEN.
© Ragne Kabanova. Shutterstock.com. Used by permission.

The temple experience is one of the most potent ways that the worldview and values of Mormon culture are strengthened. Temple rites underscore the differences between the LDS Church and other faiths, reminding people of their unique identity in the universe and in God's eternal plan.[37]

Finally, an individual's cultural identity as a Mormon is shaped by a variety of reinforcing activities built into the pattern of weekly life in the Mormon community. Members regularly observe baptisms and priesthood ordinations. They sit in weekly lessons and discussions about their history and beliefs. They often share with each other public affirmations of their convictions about the LDS Church and its most important claims.

DIVERSITY AMONG THE SAINTS

Even though we can demonstrate that Latter-day Saints are a tight-knit group sharing a common culture and identity, there is a great deal of variation within the broader Mormon culture.[38] Latter-day Saints speak of themselves as being either "active" or "inactive." (Inactive members are called "Jack-Mormons," although no one knows the origin of this label.) Even among active Mormons, some are "true believers" and others are closet doubters. Members born in the Church are different from converts.[39] Mormons living in the LDS heartland of Utah are different from those living in other places, where Saints are in the minority. Often the younger generation sees things differently from older generations.

Furthermore, Mormonism as defined by LDS Church leaders and authorities is often different from how it is lived out by average members.[40] Mormons represent different "cultural constituencies" — segments of the LDS population that define the meaning of their church membership in different ways. For some, their experience revolves around the temple, while others find their primary identity in congregational activities. Others see themselves as merely "cultural Mormons," who appreciate their LDS roots but no longer find meaning from participating in the LDS Church.[41]

INTERACTING WITH YOUR NEIGHBOR

Tradititonal Christians need to be careful about stereotyping our Latter-day Saint neighbors. We can't assume that we know a person fully simply because we have identified him or her as a Mormon. Each of us has a number of social identities. In different situations, the Mormon identity will be more or less prominent, and for some people the Mormon identity is stronger or weaker than for others. We can never assume that what is true of Mormon culture in general applies fully to each individual, nor can we assume that what is true of one group member is true of them all.[42] We can identify the most common values and experiences of Mormonism in general, but we can never know how those norms are lived out by individual members until we get to know them personally.

If Latter-day Saints are a distinct people sharing a common cultural identity, this calls for traditional Christians to interact with the

Saints in a new way. In the past, Christian churches and ministries have focused most of their attention on LDS beliefs and doctrines. Significant differences divide Mormonism from historic, biblical Christianity on a number of fundamental issues that cannot be dismissed. Yet, Latter-day Saint experience and identity goes far beyond what they believe. A young woman once asked me, "If I come to your church, do I have to stop being Mormon?" I said, "No." I understood that she was not talking about beliefs. She was asking if she had to abandon her cultural heritage.

When we limit our engagement with Mormonism to comparing truth claims, we ignore much of what matters to Mormons themselves. In large measure, the assumption has been that Latter-day Saints can be converted to the biblical gospel by convincing them, through rational arguments and proofs, that they are wrong and we are right. The problem is that people make spiritual decisions based on many other factors besides rational evaluation.

Most Latter-day Saints don't become Saints because of doctrinal considerations. They may find the belief system satisfying, but the reason they became Latter-day Saints is as likely to be relational or emotional, or simply by the circumstances of their birth. By emphasizing debates about beliefs, we treat Mormons as little more than disembodied heads, rather than as whole persons embedded in an all-encompassing culture. We need to understand and evaluate Mormonism as a culture that shapes not only the doctrines but the very identity of its people.

IS MORMONISM A CULT?

If we understand Mormonism as a cultural identity, it calls into question the wisdom of referring to the LDS Church as a "cult." Those who use the word to describe Mormonism usually have a theological definition in mind: they understand a cult as a religious group for whom the Bible is not the final authority and thus whose beliefs do not conform to biblical truth. But realistically, that's not what the word *cult* means to most people. According to one dictionary,[43] the primary definition of a cult is "a particular system of religious worship, esp. with reference to its rites and ceremonies." The sociological definition is "a group having a sacred ideology and a set of rites centering around their sacred symbols." Based on these mainstream definitions, every religious group in America is a cult.

The way most people think of the term *cult* probably reflects the dictionary's sixth entry: "a religion or sect considered to be false, unorthodox, or extremist, with members often living outside of conventional society under the direction of a charismatic leader." In popular usage, a cult is a group of strange people, out of step with normal society, brainwashed to believe and do bizarre things, and being held emotionally captive by some magnetic leader. People think of Jim Jones and his followers, who moved to Guyana to drink poisoned Kool-Aid, or Heaven's Gate, the California group who committed mass suicide in 1997 in order to join space aliens in a higher level of existence.

Those negative stereotypes — and the emotional tone associated with them — render the term *cult* to be less than useful for any meaningful discussion. It is no surprise that Latter-day Saints are offended — and the possibility of real communication is shut down — when their church is called a cult. If our goal is to have spiritual conversations with Latter-day Saints that open up opportunities to share our faith with them in a positive way, labeling them as cult members is surely unnecessary and counterproductive.

This kind of labeling leads to a narrow, inaccurate view of the LDS people. I believe that Mormonism is theologically in error, but we don't need to assign a pejorative label to sustain that claim. A false worldview lies at the heart of the Mormon culture, but Mormonism is so much more than just that worldview. It is a way of life, an identity — a learned set of values, attitudes, and behaviors that takes shape in tangible ways in social relationships, material productions, institutional structures, and more. This calls for a broader approach to faith-sharing than resorting to negative labels or merely debating our respective beliefs.

2

THE MORMON WORLDVIEW

L ATTER-DAY SAINTS HAVE many values and lifestyle practices that are
similar to traditional Christianity, but what sets Mormonism apart
most decisively is a unique worldview.[1] A worldview is a person's foundational understanding of reality. We all make assumptions, usually
not consciously or deliberately, about the natural and supernatural
worlds, humanity, time, the universe, and the purpose of existence.
Is there a God or gods? What is God like? What is the relationship of
God with everything else that exists? What is the origin, nature, and
destiny of human beings? What is the human predicament and how is
it solved? What is the meaning of this life, and what comes afterwards?
These are the components of a worldview.

The LDS view of reality is not formulated in terms familiar to traditional Christians. Mormonism is not a creedal faith. Unlike most
evangelical and mainstream Christian churches, the LDS Church has
never formalized its distinctive doctrines and teachings into a definitive statement of beliefs.[2] The identity of many traditional denomi-
nations is shaped around doctrine and in some cases is defined by
particular doctrinal disputes. Often, a person must agree with a statement of faith in order to become a member of a Christian church.
Mormonism has no such requirement. Rather, one is expected to
affirm a testimony of the truthfulness of the LDS Church, of the Book
of Mormon, and of Joseph Smith as a prophet of God. If a person

remains loyal to that affirmation, there is a great deal of room for differences in belief.

Because Latter-day Saints believe that their leaders receive continuing revelation from God, doctrine is something of a moving target. Without a definitive written creed, what was taught in a previous generation can be overturned or reinterpreted by a more recent revelation from God. Beliefs can be somewhat fluid. A fair degree of discussion is allowed among the members, within limits.[3] Saints from different generations may have different beliefs about certain matters. Recent converts or marginally active members may not fully understand or agree with commonly held beliefs. Liberal Mormons may reject some of the core assertions of the LDS Church, preferring to pick and choose their convictions.

Lacking a systematic theology, commitment is defined in social and relational terms. Latter-day Saints classify themselves as either "active" or "inactive," but never as "orthodox," "heterodox," or "heretic."[4] The LDS Church has a large body of doctrine that has been passed down from Joseph Smith and other historical leaders,[5] but this has not been codified. Some doctrines may have been emphasized more in the past than today while others are secondary matters subject to interpretation. What your LDS neighbor believes may or may not reflect the majority of Mormons, the traditional doctrines of Mormonism, or the current LDS official view.

Mormonism is a faith defined not by theological formulations but by sacred narratives. Stories — rooted in individual lives, told, experienced, believed, and supported by the collective community — have tremendous power in Mormonism.[6] The Mormon people are shaped not only by their unique beliefs but also by a sense of God's action in history.[7] The two most important stories that define how Latter-day Saints understand their place in the universe are the story of the Restoration of true Christianity and the story of humanity's potential for divine exaltation.

THE STORY OF THE RESTORATION

The story of the Restoration is the essential message the Mormons have to share with America. According to this sacred narrative, Jesus personally established his true church in ancient Palestine — as well as in the Americas — but his church fell into apostasy. After the apostles died, the authority to act for God was lost. The biblical scriptures were corrupted. The most essential elements of Jesus' work were forgotten and had to be reestablished. Hence, Mormons refer to the founding of the LDS Church as "The Restoration" — the reinstatement of true, biblical Christianity through the prophet Joseph Smith to correct the distortions that accumulated over time.[8]

The Restoration story is exciting to Latter-day Saints. The heavens are reopened after centuries of divine silence, angelic messengers reappear, holy books are rediscovered, priesthood authority is reestablished, sacred temple rites are reinauguarated, Zion is restored, and more — all in the midst of conflict and opposition.

THE HILL CUMORAH PAGEANT TELLS THE STORY OF THE COMING FORTH OF THE BOOK OF MORMON AND THE FOUNDING OF MORMONISM. © Steve Bozak. Used by permission.

The story of the Restoration is reinforced by family history. Mormons are proud of their ancestors who lived through the reestablishment of God's kingdom. They are encouraged to research family histories as a way of telling God's stories through their own life narratives. The Restoration story is told over and over in LDS artwork, recounted and celebrated through pageantry, reflected in hymnody, reenacted on Pioneer Day, and visualized in popular LDS novels and films.

The power of the Restoration story is seen in the importance of historical sites in Latter-day Saint culture. American Christians have little awareness of the history of Christianity throughout the centuries, but Latter-day Saints are thoroughly connected with their history and their roots. The LDS Church has actively sought to purchase key places in the story,[9] restoring buildings and putting up visitor centers at locations where angels appeared, where God providentially intervened, or where God's prophets lived and worked. Multitudes of Mormons have taken sacred history tours, either with private touring companies or on their own. Guides at each site provide the sacred interpretation of the events that happened there, inviting travelers to step into the story and live its meaning for themselves.

THE STORY OF SALVATION

The second essential narrative of Mormonism is grander in scope than the first — the story of the eternal progression or exaltation of humanity. Church members often call it the "Plan of Salvation" or, more recently, "The Plan of Happiness." The story extends from eternity past to eternity future, is lived out in the infinite universe, and defines the identity and purpose of the human race.[10] In traditional Christianity, the salvation story begins with the creation of all things out of nothing by a unique, eternally divine God, who alone is self-existent. After the completion of God's good creation, which climaxed with the creation of human beings, sin entered the universe through the rebellion of our first parents.

God acted to redeem his broken creation and reconcile it to himself by sending his Son to become a human being in the person of Jesus of Nazareth and to die a sacrificial death to pay for our sin. God is now at work in history establishing his kingdom through Jesus, who will one day return to remove the effects of sin, conquer all evil, and restore the original creation. Those who recognize their need and trust in Christ's saving work will experience a changed life and be united in fellowship with God forever.

The LDS story does not begin with creation. Joseph Smith did not believe that God created the universe out of nothing. Rather, the elements are as eternal and uncreated as God himself. God's act of creation was to organize what was already there. Smith taught that the human soul or intelligence — some essence of the human personality — is also without beginning. God is our Creator, not because he formed our eternal essence, but because he created spirit beings from this essence. In this sense, he is the Father of a large host of human spirits. Furthermore, we are essentially the same kind of being as him.

Joseph Smith taught that God was once a man who had a father just as we do and is a being with a physical body. He lived on a world and was taught the principles and laws that allowed him to advance to deity. In similar fashion, God offers us laws, which we can accept or reject, by which we can advance toward our destiny. This view of the universe posits a vast network of gods eternally working together to bring lesser spirits toward divine exaltation.[11]

The story of our purpose and destiny begins in premortal life, when all of God's spirit children were gathered in his presence. Latter-day Saints often call this "the Preexistence" or our "first estate." Two plans were presented for how to bring God's children to eternal salvation. Lucifer, one of God's spirit children, proposed that all would be redeemed, but no one would have a choice in the matter. This approach was rejected because it violated the principle of individual agency. Lucifer and the spirits who followed him were cast out of heaven and became the devil and his angels.[12]

The other plan, offered by Jesus, required that God's spirit children take on mortal bodies and come to this earth to be tested. This life, our "second estate," offers the opportunity to come to know the Savior, Jesus Christ, and follow his teachings — if we so choose. It is a time to develop godly attributes and wisdom through work and discipline, with the goal of returning to Heavenly Father again and starting on the path of eternal progression.[13] Those who did not have an opportunity in this life to fulfill the ordinances necessary to progress will have a second chance in the life to come. Before the final judgment, they will hear about God's plan and have the ordinances performed on their behalf by those who are still on this earth — which they can then accept or reject.[14]

Joseph Smith taught that heaven encompasses three degrees of eternal glory. The highest level, called the celestial kingdom, lies open to those who live up to the requisite laws and ordinances in this life. Those who do not measure up go to one of the lower levels of heaven. Latter-day Saints don't believe in the traditional concept of hell. To them, "damnation" means that eternal progress is no longer possible.[15] But in the celestial kingdom, human beings can continue to develop. As Lorenzo Snow, the fifth LDS Church President, put it, "As Man is, God once was; as God is, Man may become."[16] The idea that men may become gods of other worlds is currently played down by Latter-day Saints in public discourse. Sources now talk about becoming "like God" rather than becoming gods, but the principle of eternal progression toward exaltation remains the cornerstone of the Mormon worldview.[17]

This grand vision of progress to godhood is not seen as an individual journey. Joseph Smith envisioned binding the generations of humanity together forever in an unbroken chain.[18] As God joins his spirit children to himself in the journey to exaltation, it is widely accepted that a Heavenly Mother stands beside him, although official sources typically speak generically of "heavenly parents." Their spirit children, obeying the foundational laws and principles, likewise can become heavenly parents to their own families of spirit children. In other words, eternal progression occurs in family units, not alone.[19]

Latter-day Saints don't speculate a lot about eternity past, about what gods existed before Heavenly Father, where everything came from, how the chain of progression began in the first place, how raw intelligence was formed into individual human spirits, or what the preexistence was like. Nor do they speculate about how exaltation works in the world to come. The most important part of the story for the Saints is this moment on earth. Having stepped out of God's presence and into the challenges of mortal life, will they choose the right? Will they be able, in the face of life's temptations, to return to their Father in heaven?

In daily practice, this worldview translates into an emphasis on proving worthy. With a strong disposition toward perfectionism, Mormons are great achievers. The virtues of hard work and self-reliance are not only rooted in the pioneer experience but in the promise of exaltation, which depends on mastering the principles that govern the universe.[20] As a result, Mormons may have a strong sense of purpose and a strong confidence in their eternal identity. They may come across with such confidence about their eternal potential that they appear arrogant. Yet, many also have doubts about how well they measure up.[21] As we will see, active Saints place tremendous emphasis on the temple, because this view of the universe is reinforced in the scripts and rituals of the temple rite.

WHO DEFINES MORMON BELIEFS?

Christians from the historic biblical tradition will recognize that this worldview is not derived from biblical sources alone. It was developed by Joseph Smith in his revelations, his speeches, and in the scriptures he introduced. This raises the issue of what Latter-day Saints view as authoritative sources of truth. The question becomes practical when you have a conversation with a Mormon because your friend may not accept your understanding of what Mormonism teaches. With considerable

ambiguity about what constitutes official doctrine, theological speculation has never been rare among the Mormons, often going far beyond
mainstream Church teaching.[22]
Who or what, then, defines LDS
beliefs?

JOSEPH SMITH'S TEACHINGS ARE CENTRAL
TO LDS BELIEFS. © Utah State Historical Society,
all rights reserved. Used by permission.

Sociologist Armand Mauss
suggests a hierarchy of authoritative
sources,[23] starting with the LDS
scriptures at the top. These include
the four "standard works": the Bible,
the Book of Mormon, the Doctrine
and Covenants, and the Pearl of
Great Price. Although the Bible is
received as divine scripture, Latter-
day Saints view it as inaccurate
and incomplete, having been cor-
rupted during the great apostasy.[24] The Book of Mormon claims to be
an ancient record reporting the spiritual history of the nations that once
inhabited the Americas.[25] The Doctrine and Covenants is a collection
of modern revelations, mostly those of Joseph Smith. The Pearl of Great
Price contains books that Saints believe were written by the ancient
prophets Moses and Abraham, along with the official account of Joseph
Smith's early prophetic work.[26]

Still authoritative, but less so than the standard scriptures, are official
statements by the Church and its highest leaders. The words of Joseph
Smith are at the top of this list,[27] followed by statements of current
prophets, Church lesson manuals, and official policy handbooks, magazines, and other publications. These are recognized as official doctrine
when they are presented, with the understanding that doctrine may
change over time as God reveals further truths. Considered somewhat
less authoritative are all the other speeches, teachings, and publications
of other Church authorities on various doctrines and scriptures.

The lowest and least authoritative source of truth for Latter-day Saints would be what I call "folk Mormonism," the broad collection of commonly believed teachings and practices perpetuated orally over time but not necessarily recorded in official sources.[28] Along with their scriptures and the teachings of Church leaders, Latter-day Saints look to personal revelation to know what is true. Beliefs and teachings are personally appropriated by the Saints through experiences and feelings that they believe come from God.[29]

INTERACTING WITH YOUR NEIGHBOR

Clearly, key elements of the foundational LDS stories are at odds with historic biblical Christianity. We reject their claim of total apostasy. As one studies how the Bible was transmitted from ancient manuscripts to contemporary translations, there is no evidence that the Bible was corrupted. In fact, the evidence is that the biblical text was remarkably preserved over time. Biblical passages that talk about apostasy refer to future events, not past. History shows that there have always been faithful followers of Jesus on the earth, demonstrating that God has the power to preserve what he started.

The LDS plan of salvation is a fairly coherent system. Given its basic assumptions, the LDS story makes sense and has elements that people find compelling. Most Latter-day Saints don't dwell on the prospect of becoming gods, but many of them find meaning in the opportunity to be tested and found worthy, stirred by the underlying principles of achievement and advancement. While it leaves much up to speculation, it also provides satisfying answers to a number of questions — such as the fate of those who have never heard about Jesus.

Nonetheless, traditional Christians must respectfully question key elements of the story. We cannot accept the idea that God was once a man or that humanity is eternal. God is a transcendent being who has always been divine. By contrast, we are finite beings who have always been creatures. We cannot believe that matter is eternal and uncreated. We do not see the universe as subject to control and conquest by human beings as they apply the laws and principles that govern it. We believe there is only one heaven, inhabited by those who trust fully and solely in the sacrifice Jesus made on the cross to pay for our sins and reconcile us to God. The human destiny is not to become gods but to enjoy relationship with God in an evil-free existence for eternity.

As you develop a relationship with your LDS neighbor and have opportunity to discuss these worldviews, you will soon realize that Latter-day Saints think about truth differently than traditional Christians. We tend to emphasize the authority of the Bible. Latter-day Saints emphasize other authorities and typically use the Bible when it supports those other sources. We often rely on rational evidences and lines of reasoning to make our case for the existence of God, the resurrection of Jesus, or the reliability of the Bible. While Latter-day Saints refer to evidences for their beliefs, they place a great deal of emphasis on having a spiritual experience whereby God validates the truth personally and subjectively.

I was talking to one young LDS man on a college campus. He said, "I don't care if you could prove to me that Joseph Smith is not a prophet of God. I know without a doubt that the Mormon Church is true" — based on his spiritual experience. It's not that Saints don't use their minds or that traditional Christians don't have spiritual experiences that confirm truth for them, but the relative weight placed on different forms of evidence is different.

Historic Christians don't simply disagree with Mormons about the nature of the world, God, humanity, and salvation. Rather, we disagree on the very source of truth. It's fair to say that in practice, the final authority for active Mormons is the LDS Church. It is the Church that presents and interprets the scriptures for its people and that mediates divine revelation from God.

3

THE ONE TRUE CHURCH

T HE CHURCH OF Jesus Christ of Latter-day Saints professes to be the very church that Jesus himself established when he was on the earth. It claims to have the same doctrine, organization, and authority as Jesus' original church. Mormons see their Church as "the only true and living church upon the face of the earth."[1] They call it simply "the Church" — shorthand for its entire history, doctrine, practice, and organization.[2]

Active Latter-day Saints typically have a more extensive relationship with their church than most traditional Christians. The Church has unique status to them. Membership is formal and serious compared to Protestant groups.[3] Active Latter-day Saints don't just "go to church." The Church is central to all of life. If asked who they are, many Saints rank their church affiliation above race, class, or vocation. They invest deeply in the requirements of church membership. Many contribute 10 percent of their annual income to the Church. They may work ten or fifteen hours a week in unpaid service to the Church. Mormons feel immensely loyal to the institution of the Church.[4]

NO SALVATION WITHOUT THE CHURCH

Mainstream and evangelical Christians view the local church as a way to live in community with like-minded believers. To Latter-day Saints, the LDS Church is much more than that. The Church is the matrix in which salvation is achieved. The Church teaches the correct principles that guide a person to happiness. The Church provides the opportunity to learn the eternal principles that ensure joy in the next world.[5] Without the Church's ordinances, performed by the Church's authority, a person cannot attain the highest levels of salvation. The Church and its ordinances provide the only valid context for exaltation.[6]

The LDS Church has long been clear about its three main purposes:[7]

1. "to proclaim the gospel of the Lord Jesus Christ to every nation, kindred, tongue and people"
2. "to perfect the saints by preparing them to receive the ordinances of the gospel and by instruction and discipline to gain exaltation"
3. "to redeem the dead by performing vicarious ordinances of the gospel for those who have lived on the Earth"

The LDS Church, then, sees itself as the vehicle of salvation for those on earth (who need to hear the message), for those who have already joined the Church (who need to become perfected), and for those who have died (who need ordinances performed for them to advance to the highest heaven). A fourth purpose has recently been added: to care for the poor and needy — which the Church has been doing for many years.[8]

CONTINUING REVELATION

One of the exclusive claims Mormons make about their Church is that it is the only church governed by ongoing revelation from God. Its leaders are not merely executives or teachers; they are apostles and prophets of God, equivalent to the biblical apostles and prophets of old. They believe that the Church's President, Thomas S. Monson, is a "prophet, seer, and revelator," meaning that he receives revelation from God to direct the affairs of the Church.

Latter-day Saints hold their prophets in high regard.[9] They will travel many miles for an opportunity to see one of the Church's prophets or apostles in person. Joseph Smith in particular is revered by Mormons. The LDS Church hymnal contains a popular hymn called "Praise to the Man," in which Smith is extolled for his role in bringing original Christianity back to the earth.[10] While Smith is the most revered, faithful Mormons venerate each of their Presidents. The current leader is referred to simply as "the Prophet" and is heeded and followed as the Lord's spokesman.[11]

PRAISE TO THE MAN

Praise to the man who communed with Jehovah!
Jesus anointed that Prophet and Seer.
Blessed to open the last dispensation,
Kings shall extol him, and nations revere.
Chorus

Hail to the Prophet, ascended to heaven!
Traitors and tyrants now fight him in vain.
Mingling with Gods, he can plan for his brethren;
Death cannot conquer the hero again.

Praise to his mem'ry, he died as a martyr;
Honored and blest be his ever great name!
Long shall his blood, which was shed by assassins,
Plead unto heav'n while the earth lauds his fame.
Chorus

Great is his glory and endless his priesthood.
Ever and ever the keys he will hold.
Faithful and true he will enter his kingdom,
Crowned in the midst of the prophets of old.
Chorus

Sacrifice brings forth the blessings of heaven;
Earth must atone for the blood of that man.
Wake up the world for the conflict of justice.
Millions shall know "Brother Joseph" again.
Chorus

Because it is guided by continuing revelation, Mormonism has proven to be fluid and dynamic, adapting to changing cultural conditions. One LDS writer, explaining why the Church no longer practices polygamy, says: "The Church is able to free itself of historical precedent if change is revealed to the Prophet."[12] In talking to Latter-day Saints about their beliefs, it helps to remember that not everything prophets taught in the past is considered authoritative today. It is fruitless to bring up issues that contemporary Mormons do not hold to, even if they were emphasized at one time.

PRIESTHOOD AUTHORITY

The LDS Church claims to have the original biblical priesthood. The priesthood keys — the right to exercise power in the name of Jesus Christ to preside over the functions of the Church — were restored to Joseph Smith after the apostasy.[13]

Priesthood holders lead the LDS Church by wielding both administrative and spiritual authority. Only priesthood holders are authorized to administer saving ordinances of the Church such as baptism, imparting the gift of the Holy Ghost, and ordaining others to the priesthood. The temple rites that give worthy members the authority to enter into the highest levels of heaven are administered by the priesthood.[14] No ordinance is valid before God unless it is performed by a priesthood holder in good standing.[15]

While priesthood keys are required to lead the Church and perform its ordinances, priesthood also has a dynamic function in the individual lives of Latter-day Saints. Priesthood holders are empowered to give special blessings when times of trial take place, when there is sickness, when new responsibilities are accepted, or whenever spiritual guidance is desired.[16]

The priesthood is open to all male members. Boys are typically ordained to the Aaronic Priesthood at age twelve. The Melchizedek Priesthood is held by men, who are most often ordained to this level of priesthood, with its greater authority and privileges, prior to going on a mission. They can advance within the Melchizedek Priesthood as they are given additional responsibilities in the Church.[17]

THE CHURCH'S GOVERNING HIERARCHY

The LDS Church is governed by a group of men called General Authorities: priesthood leaders who administer the Church's programs around the world.[18] Since they possess the priesthood and continuing revelation, the General Authorities wield a great deal of power. They are regarded as Christ's representatives over both the spiritual and temporal affairs of the Church.[19] The ultimate leader of the Church is its President, who is assisted by two counselors. These three constitute the First Presidency, which along with the Quorum of the Twelve Apostles below them forms the highest level of church leadership.[20]

Organized under the First Presidency and the Twelve Apostles are the Quorums of the Seventy, senior leaders who represent the prophet and the apostles around the world and implement their policies.[21] The final group of General Authorities is the Presiding Bishopric, a panel of three men who supervise the Church's earthly concerns, such as building programs and financial management.[22] The Church also appoints teams of women to lead its women's and children's auxiliaries. Even though their assignments give them worldwide responsibility, they are

THE LDS CHURCH IS GOVERNED FROM THE
CHURCH OFFICE BUILDING IN DOWNTOWN
SALT LAKE CITY, UTAH. © Ross Anderson.

not considered part of the General Authorities because women do not hold the LDS priesthood.[23] The activities of the Church are implemented by a bureaucracy of career employees who work in Church institutions, such as the Family History Library, the welfare program, architectural services, and the Church's education system.[24]

As centralized and hierarchical as the LDS Church is, at the local level it is highly democratic. Mormonism has no professional pastors or priests at the local level.[25] Each congregation is led entirely by volunteers. The authority given to local members, coupled with the broad distribution of priesthood to all worthy males and an emphasis on personal revelation, creates an egalitarian impulse in Mormonism.

Yet the supreme spiritual authority rests at the top of the hierarchy.[26] Mormonism places a great deal of emphasis on the principle of "free agency," the freedom and responsibility of individuals to make meaningful choices for themselves as they seek God's guidance. Yet, "the church Joseph founded is one of the most centralized, hierarchical, authoritarian churches in America."[27] The General Authorities are all-powerful within the Church. The members have no say in decisions made at the top.[28] Latter-day Saints do not like to be accused of blind obedience to their leaders, but they are, for the most part, ready to follow orders.[29]

The interplay between free agency and divine authority creates a tension within Mormonism — and often within individual Mormons.

Some Saints find comfort and safety in holding fast to the authority of the Prophet and the Church. Others find freedom in the principle of individual agency, which they see as the vehicle of personal growth. The one group will be suspicious of independent thinking as an expression of pride and potential rebellion while the other will see unquestioning obedience as a failure to exercise one's own moral responsibility.[30]

THE CHURCH IN MEMBERS' LIVES

The average Latter-day Saint lives out his or her life within the context of a local congregation, called a "ward." Several wards make up a "stake." Members also participate directly in the broader Church in a variety of ways. The Church holds its General Conference twice each year, in April and October. Saints from everywhere gather in Salt Lake City to receive instruction and inspiration from the General Authorities. Although the General Conference is broadcast by satellite to LDS chapels, attending

BRIGHAM YOUNG UNIVERSITY IS THE LARGEST PRIVATE, CHURCH-SPONSORED UNIVERSITY IN THE UNITED STATES. © Ken Lund. Used by permission via Creative Commons.

Conference in person can be a once-in-a-lifetime pilgrimage filled with cherished experiences.[31] Messages presented by the General Authorities are considered almost on a par with scripture. They are published in Church magazines and used in lesson manuals.[32]

The Church publishes one principal magazine called *The Ensign*, along with *The New Era* for youth and *The Friend* for children. The *LDS Church News* reports faith-promoting stories from the Church's activities around the world. These can all be subscribed to in print or accessed online. The website www.lds.org presents an extensive library of resources, curriculum, Church magazines, and much more, for members of the Church.

A large influx of converts to Mormonism in the second half of the twentieth century led Church leaders to try to simplify and coordinate the Church's programs. Known as "Correlation," this effort involved centralized control over ward activities, organizational structures, planning, and teaching materials.[33] Sunday school classes, youth, and children's groups all use the materials developed and furnished by the Church.

Most members will have some interaction with the Church Educational System (CES). Academic advancement is driven by a statement in the Doctrine and Covenants that "the glory of God is intelligence."[34] CES operates a training system for high school and college students. High school students attend seminary. In Utah and several other states, seminary is offered during the school day as a "released time" class. Elsewhere, Mormon teens get up early and attend seminary before their first high school class of the day. Each year's curriculum focuses on one of the Church's standard scriptures: the Book of Mormon, the Doctrine and Covenants, the Old Testament, and the New Testament.

The Institute of Religion offers classes for college students. The Church usually acquires a building near a college campus, which serves as a social center as well as a religious training environment. The Institute offers classes in all the LDS scriptures, the writings of modern LDS prophets, Mormon Church history, marriage, and missionary preparation.[35]

The Church also operates Brigham Young University (BYU). BYU's main campus in Provo, Utah, is the largest private, church-sponsored university in the United States, with around 35,000 students studying in nearly 200 bachelors, 68 masters, and 27 doctoral programs.[36] BYU operates smaller affiliated campuses in Rexburg, Idaho, and Laie, Hawaii.

Most members will interact at some point with LDS Welfare Services, an extensive system maintained to help members in financial need. Volunteers from local wards donate thousands of hours to the welfare system every year, working at church-owned farms, canning plants, and manufacturing facilities to provide food and essential goods to members with short-term needs.[37] Resources are dispensed from over 140 storehouses to help those going through unemployment, illness, or family breakups to become self-sufficient.[38] Recipients typically donate time or skills in exchange for help.

FOOD FOR NEEDY CHURCH MEMBERS IS PRODUCED AND PROCESSED IN LARGE QUANTITIES AT WELFARE SQUARE IN SALT LAKE CITY. Anonymous. Used by permission.

Latter-day Saints promote recreation as an essential aspect of church life.[39] Most of this is implemented at the ward and stake levels, including music, dance, drama, speech, sports, and visual arts.[40] Youth are the primary focus of recreation programs. The Especially for Youth conference gathers teens from different regions to share cultural and spiritual experiences, including dances, parties, talent shows, workshops, and worship meetings.[41]

INTERACTING WITH YOUR NEIGHBOR

Traditional Christian churches don't accept the unique claims of the LDS Church. Most believe that Jesus is the final revelation of God (Hebrews 1:1 – 2) and that the Bible, as the reflection and expression of that revelation, is sufficient for whatever God wants us to know and do. Though some Christians believe God provides daily guidance at a personal level, this is not considered comparable to scripture nor is it authoritative for others.

The Bible teaches that all Christ-followers are priests of God (1 Peter 3:9 – 10). We don't need a special priesthood ordination to act in God's name. Our authority is inherent in God's command. If your boss tells you to finish a project, that command implies the delegated authority to do it. The same applies to God's commands to us to baptize, pray for healing, and so forth. Our authority is also inherent in our relationship with God. Those who trust in Jesus become God's children. As such, we bear the authority of our Father.

In addition, the LDS description of the Aaronic and Melchizedek priesthoods doesn't match how the Bible describes those priesthoods. In the Bible, the Aaronic priesthood has the authority to administer the Old Testament sacrificial system, which no longer functions since the sacrificial system has been fulfilled in Christ. Moreover, the only person who meets the qualifications for the Melchizedek priesthood is Jesus Christ himself (Hebrews 7:23 – 26). Traditional Christian churches don't see the LDS priesthood as reflecting the biblical concept of priesthood in any way.

Evangelicals don't claim that their church is the one true church on earth. We all believe largely the same foundational beliefs (with differences in style and in nonessential matters). We also subscribe to a different vision of what the church Jesus founded is like. The New Testament presents local congregations as people who share life in Christ together, led by people they have chosen to shepherd and serve them. Beyond each local church, the New Testament views the larger, universal church as consisting of all people everywhere who are united to each other spiritually by virtue of their being united to Jesus by faith in him — regardless of their denominational membership. The church is described by New Testament writers in organic rather than institutional terms: as a living body, a flock, a family. Where offices are mentioned, they often refer to functions in the local congregation.

Mormonism reads its organizational structure backwards into the New Testament, to see connections that aren't really there. Beyond a superficial similarity of titles, the church described in the New Testament is in no way similar to the hierarchical, centralized LDS Church of our day. For example, there is no evidence that the Seventy sent out by Jesus (Luke 10:1) to declare God's kingdom ever became a formal office or even existed beyond the end of Jesus' earthly ministry. The Latter-day Saint office of deacon is held by teenaged boys, while the New Testament describes deacons as married men.[42] The biblical picture of the apostles does not show them exercising centralized governing authority over the entire Christian movement as it spread throughout the Roman world.

It is easy to see why the LDS Church is so important to its members. Evangelical Christians attend church based on their affinity with the beliefs, style, and ministries of a local congregation, often with little concern for denominational affiliation. Many of us switch churches with relative ease when moving to a new town or passing through a new stage of life. Latter-day Saints see their church as far more than just another good denomination. It is the only church that possesses everything needed to be fully saved or exalted.

Mormons see the religious world in somewhat black and white terms, which explains why they are so keen to convert others to Mormonism — even those who already attend another church. They believe that your church may have a lot of truth and do many excellent things, but it will never possess the authority of the priesthood or be guided by a living prophet. Your LDS neighbor believes you need to leave your church and join the one true Church in order to fully follow Jesus Christ.

4

LIFE IN THE LOCAL CONGREGATION

THE LDS WARD has similiarities with other religious congregations. Its members pray, sing, baptize, give talks, read sacred scriptures, eat and drink sacred elements, make friends, and bear testimony of their religious experience.[1] The ward — a self-contained local congregation of 300 to 400 members — is the primary environment where Latter-day Saints experience community with their peers. In areas lacking sufficient members or resources, the Church organizes smaller congregations called "branches," which do not offer the complete program.[2]

As Mormons moved from Utah to relocate in other parts of America, local wards became the cultural centers for LDS life. Wards created a context for mutual accountability, support, counseling, and friendship. The ward, with its extensive programs, replaced the village life of Utah.[3] Community had been a region; now it became a local congregation.

Wherever you go throughout America, wards are much the same. The larger Church dictates the ward's leadership, boundaries, and programs. Wards follow the same schedule and incorporate most of the same programs and experiences. There are differences between wards due to unique personalities, various educational and economic levels, different ethnic composition, and particular history. Since the general format is the same, the impression is created that the LDS Church is the same everywhere.[4]

A TYPICAL LDS MEETING HOUSE. © Ross Anderson.

In a typical Protestant congregation, members choose which congregation they will join and may drive past similar churches to attend the church of their choice. By contrast, LDS wards are defined by particular geographical boundaries and members are expected to attend the ward in which they reside. There are exceptions. University students may attend wards organized for students. Single adults may attend special singles wards in lieu of their geographical wards. At times, wards and branches are created for non-English speakers.[5] When ward membership becomes too large, new wards are created by realigning the boundaries. Typically two or three wards will share a single building on Sundays by meeting at different times.[6]

THE WARD CHAPEL

Buildings where wards meet are called "churches" or "chapels." Ward chapels have essentially the same format and style everywhere in America, at least since the mid-twentieth century. The standard floor plan is practical. The auditorium, where the main Sunday services are held, is attractive but plain, usually in natural wood tones with no religious ornamentation.[7] LDS buildings do not display the cross in the auditorium or anywhere on the building. Simple pews face a raised platform, which contains seating for a choir and for those leading and participating in the service. On one side of the platform is a simple table used for the bread and water of the weekly "sacrament," a ritual similar to the Lord's Supper in traditional Christian churches.[8]

Most ward chapels have a "cultural hall," an open hall used for sports, stage productions, and social gatherings.[9] The auditorium and cultural hall are separated only by a movable curtain, which allows for overflow seating. These two central rooms are surrounded by class-rooms.[10] The building usually has a baptismal font. Ward officials have offices there and the facility is used throughout the week for a variety of meetings and activities.[11]

HOW A WARD IS GOVERNED

Each ward is led by a bishop appointed by the Church hierarchy to act as the administrative and spiritual leader of the ward, in some ways like a traditional pastor. Along with his counselors, a bishop will supervise Sunday services and ward activities, manage the ward's extensive volunteer ministries, oversee welfare projects and disburse-ments, maintain discipline, and counsel individual members. Bishops continue to work full-time in their secular jobs, receiving no com-pensation from their congregations or the central Church.[12] A bishop must be an adult male, since women cannot be ordained to the priest-hood. He will serve approximately five years, after which he can be reassigned to any other position of service in the ward.[13]

One of the bishop's responsibilities is discipline. He interviews people to determine their worthiness prior to priesthood advance-ment, a mission calling, or admittance to the temple. The bishop may initiate contact with those who are not living up to their member-ship commitments. When necessary, he may convene a disciplinary court to restore fallen members. Excommunication may be imposed, although the goal is correction and improvement rather than expulsion. The bishop's power is limited to the dealings of the local ward. He is answerable to the Stake President and ultimately to the Church hierarchy, culminating in the First Presidency.[14]

The bishop also assigns members to fill the numerous positions in the ward's organizational structure, be it a Sunday school teacher, scoutmaster, or clerk. He prayerfully considers available candidates for each task before issuing a "call" for a person to serve. The individual called seeks divine guidance before assenting to the assignment, but a call issued by the bishop is seldom declined.[15] A visit from the bishop is rarely a social occasion and likely signals another call to duty.[16] Mormons are expected to give great amounts of time in serving the Church. The Saints believe that God directs the bishop, so when a call is issued or a change of assignment is made, they see it as God's will.[17]

THE AUXILIARIES

The functions of each ward are carried out through priesthood groups and "auxiliary" organizations for women, youth, and children. Volunteers also staff Sunday school, youth programs, family history research, music, and more.

Priesthood holders are organized into quorums. The Aaronic Priesthood is divided by age into three groups of young men: deacons, teachers, and priests. These quorums are led by adult teachers and advisors and each has its own presidency made up of worthy young men. Melchizedek priesthood holders meet in either the elder's quorum or the high priest's quorum. These groups are a forum for instruction, discussion, and training. Service projects are organized and recurring duties are assigned. One important function of the priesthood quorums is "home teaching," a program by which the membership of the ward is divided up and every member is visited each month by a team of two priesthood holders.

The organization for women is called the Relief Society. The women meet each Sunday for an hour that includes prayers, songs, and a short lesson. They also gather for a monthly "enrichment" meeting,[18] along with several times throughout the year in combined meetings with the Relief Societies in the same stake. The Relief Society provides friendships, trains women with life skills, and organizes service projects. The women visit other women each month in a program called "visiting teaching."[19] Women have influence even though they cannot be ordained to the priesthood. They run the auxiliary organizations for women, teenage girls, and children. They pray and teach in mixed meetings and are encouraged to seek revelation from God for their own lives and ministries, just as men are.[20]

Children are served through the Primary, a Sunday school program with classes each Sunday for three- to twelve-year-olds. Children learn the stories of the Bible and the Book of Mormon. Lessons are reinforced with music, skits, and class projects. Older elementary students also meet in after-school activities during the week, such as Cub Scouts.[21]

Youth are organized in parallel groups called Young Women and Young Men. They meet in classes on Sundays and also attend an activity

THE LDS CHURCH SPONSORS MORE BOY SCOUT TROOPS THAN ANY OTHER AGENCY. © Sandi Mako. Shutterstock.com. Used by permission.

night each week, which may include short lessons, skill workshops, service projects, and recreational games.[22] Teenage boys attend Boy Scout activities, reflecting a long-standing partnership between the LDS Church and the Boy Scouts of America.[23]

WHAT HAPPENS ON SUNDAYS

The centerpiece of the ward's community life is the block of Sunday meetings. For active Latter-day Saints, church attendance on Sundays is not optional.[24] Of all the major religious traditions in America, Mormons are the most active in attending religious services. Over three-quarters say they attend church at least once a week, compared to 39 percent among the general population.[25] At Sunday gatherings, members usually wear "Sunday best" clothing, which means shirts and ties for men and dresses or skirts for women.[26]

When the Saints gather at the chapel on Sunday, they expect to be in meetings for about three hours, with time before and after for appointments or informal fellowship. Most of the meetings of the various auxiliaries are consolidated into this block. When different wards meet in the same building, they rotate each year between an earlier or a later schedule.

Sacrament Meeting — the LDS worship service — comes first. The meeting begins with an opening hymn sung from the LDS hymnal, usually accompanied by piano or organ, followed by an opening prayer. Prayer is addressed to "Heavenly Father" in the name of Jesus Christ. The person praying ends with an "Amen," which is echoed reverently by the congregation. Early in the service, there is usually some ward business, which might include announcement of events, introduction of people with new callings, and the release of others from existing callings.

At the heart of Sacrament Meeting is the sacrament service, the LDS version of the Lord's Supper. Broken bread and tiny cups of water are prepared and distributed by teenage Aaronic priesthood holders as a more solemn hymn is sung. These elements represent the body of Christ and his atoning blood.[27] As members eat the elements, they reflect on the covenants they made to God in their baptism and on the promise of forgiveness for the repentant. Reverent silence is encouraged.[28]

After the sacrament, several members of the ward — including teens — might give short inspirational messages. These talks are five to fifteen minutes long and usually reflect on moral principles and life experiences consistent with the LDS scriptures. The main speaker might be the bishop, one of his counselors, a returning missionary, or an official visiting from the stake or regional hierarchy. No offering is received during Sacrament Meeting.[29] Mormons strongly emphasize tithing, but they never pass an offering plate. Instead, members typically give their offering in an envelope to the bishop. The meeting closes with another hymn and prayer.[30]

When Sacrament Meeting is over, the congregation is dismissed to Sunday school. Teens and children go to age-segregated classes. Most adults attend the "Gospel Doctrine" class. During the third hour of the block, men attend priesthood quorum meetings while women go to Relief Society. Teens go to the Young Men's and Young Women's groups and children attend Primary.[31]

FAST AND TESTIMONY MEETING

On the first Sunday of each month, Sacrament Meeting takes a different twist. This Sunday is set aside as a day of fasting and prayer. Members typically go without two meals and donate the money they would have spent on food to the Church to help the poor. Sacrament Meeting becomes "Fast and Testimony Meeting."[32] On this Sunday, babies are blessed and newly baptized members are confirmed. In place of the regular Sacrament Meeting talks, members bear their testimonies. One at a time, they spontaneously go to the podium to give thanks for personal blessings, talk about faith-promoting experiences, and affirm their confidence in the truth of Mormon claims.[33]

Members declare that they know the LDS Church is true, that Joseph Smith was a prophet of God, that the current Church president is a prophet, that the Book of Mormon is true, or similar affirmations about the core principles of the Restoration. These monthly testimonies reinforce the speaker's identification with the history and beliefs of the group while bolstering the confidence of those listening. Often testimony bearing is an emotional experience, accompanied by faltering voice and tears.[34]

While Fast and Testimony Meeting can be a moving experience, Sacrament Meeting in general lacks the sense of transcendence that most traditional Christians associate with worship. In the biblical Christian worldview, God is infinitely above and distinct from his creation, but the LDS worldview collapses the distance between God and human beings. One LDS scholar, commenting on the implications for artists of a God who is the same kind of being as us, writes:

> If God is shorn of ineffability and transcendence, or is construed in human terms, how does one find the reverential awe that moves one to true worshipfulness? If Jesus is our "big brother," how can he be our Lord and God? Reverence before the Almighty must be freshly conceptualized in such a reconfigured heaven and earth. But the dilemmas for the artist are especially vexing: in a universe devoid of transcendence and sacred distance (at least as conventionally constructed), how can wonder flourish?[35]

INVITE YOUR NEIGHBOR TO WORSHIP

I believe that human beings are created to worship a transcendent God. An experience of true worship can speak to the LDS heart. Encountering the infinite God in worship can awaken their natural yearning for something greater than themselves. I recommend inviting your LDS friend to attend a worship service with you.

You should also consider attending Sacrament Meeting. Go with your neighbor, observe what happens, and ask questions about what you see. If anything, this will open more dialog as you take a genuine interest in entering your friend's life. As part of that dialog, it opens the door for your friend to reciprocate by attending a worship service with you.

Before you invite, here are some things to consider. Latter-day Saints are often reticent about attending another church. Start with an interdenominational worship gathering or a concert at a neutral site. If you attend a church service, be sure the church you are going to is not going to denigrate Mormonism publicly. Often well-meaning pastors and church members do this without thinking. Don't introduce your friend as a Mormon because people will not know how to respond and may say something insensitive.

Latter-day Saints are not accustomed to more energetic and highly expressive worship styles since their meetings are orderly and reverent. They may be put off by some of the practices common in some churches. Pastors in Utah call this the "cringe factor." If you invite, put yourself in your friend's shoes. The idea is to expose him or her to an authentic experience of transcendence before the living God. Avoid situations where things happen that a Latter-day Saint would find strange or confusing.

To some extent, this will depend on your friend. Since Sacrament Meeting features piano and organ, some Saints will find it strange to hear a contemporary band leading worship, though some might find it interesting and refreshing. Many churches serve coffee. An active Mormon might find this offensive, but most are used to the prevalence of coffee in American life and will not be bothered. Many churches emphasize casual dress while Latter-day Saints are used to "Sunday best," which might be an obstacle for some. Explain in advance to your neighbor the elements that are different from Sacrament Meeting.

RELATIONSHIPS IN THE WARD

Because the ward functions as a primary community for Latter-day Saints, relationships in the ward are strong and highly valued. The ward is not simply a church. It is a community and social center. The variety of ward activities creates strong social networks.[36] The custom of ward members to call each other "Brother Jones" or "Sister Smith" reinforces the sense of connectedness within the ward as a community.[37] Close-knit wards can become like an extended family for ward members.[38] In times of emotional stress, the ward provides a safety net.[39]

On the flip side, however, the ward community can be so tight-knit that members may have little empathy for or understanding of nonmembers. If one's social life centers around the ward, the ward can become a cocoon. An active Saint may not feel the need for outside friendships, while inactive members may feel ignored. In Utah, wards are geographically small and coincide with neighborhoods. This often leaves nonmembers and inactives feeling left out, as if one has to be an active member of the ward to fit in the neighborhood community.

FOURTH OF JULY CHARITY BREAKFAST AT AN LDS WARD. © Jeremy O. Evans. Used by permission.

While LDS wards form a close community, the ward does not necessarily create the conditions for intimacy between people. The personal interaction in the ward is often functional, focused on getting work done. The level of common beliefs and culture can lead people to feel comfortable in the community without deep relationships. Because of the emphasis on being faithful or active, conformity and participation can be valued more than transparency. As an acquaintance of mine once said, "You can get a casserole when you're sick, but not when you're doubting." Because of expectations to maintain a strong testimony and to appear active, Latter-day Saints will not share their most intimate questions and needs with others in their ward. I have found that as we as evangelicals develop gracious and trusting relationships with Mormons, they may turn to us with some of their deepest challenges.

5

FAMILIES ARE FOREVER

FAMILY LIES AT the heart of LDS beliefs and values. The LDS view of family is deeply rooted beneath the visible surface of their large families and conservative values in a unique worldview. The family unit is sacred. Heaven is seen as an extension of home life on this earth, where families can exist intact forever.[1] Mormonism presents a universe that is organized along family lines, wherein humans are the literal spirit children of a heavenly father and mother. Creating families is the central purpose of earthly life. Through families, God brings his spirit children to this earth to obtain bodies and learn correct principles.[2] Only in families can they progress to the highest degree of salvation in the world to come.[3] The very essence of exaltation is the power to reproduce life eternally, through marriage and procreation, within the context of a forever family.[4]

The eternal family lineage stretches backward as well as forward. Mormonism emphasizes a bond between the living and their deceased relatives, which is why active Latter-day Saints pursue genealogy to collect the names of their ancestors in order to perform essential ordinances by proxy for them. They have a role in providing salvation for their forebears, creating a sort of "family tree of salvation."[5] Genealogical records are so important to the LDS Church that they store vast holdings of such records in carefully monitored environmental conditions in a giant vault in the mountains overlooking Salt Lake City.[6]

MORMON FAMILY VALUES

Family values and practices arise out of this family-centered view of the world. Social research has identified four areas where LDS family life differs measurably from mainstream America.[7] First, Mormons are more conservative about sexual behavior before marriage. Sexuality is valued as an expression of love and commitment between eternal partners. It is the means God uses to bring spirit children out of the preexistence into this mortal world and has the power to create an eternally increasing family. Sexual activity outside of marriage is forbidden, including homosexuality, premarital sex, adultery, and pornography. Masturbation is strongly discouraged. Young people are encouraged to remain chaste until marriage and to marry early in order to develop their sexuality within the proper boundaries.[8]

Second, Mormons are more likely to marry and less likely to divorce. Not all Mormons marry or stay married but nearly three-quarters of Mormons are married, compared to just more than half among the general population.[9] Marriage is so strongly encouraged that an

MORMONS ARE KNOWN FOR HAVING LARGE FAMILIES. © Jaren Jai Wicklund. Shutterstock.com. Used by permission.

unmarried man approaching age thirty will raise questions. Women are given the benefit of the doubt, but men are strongly expected to do what it takes to find a mate. To encourage this, the Church organizes young adults in urban areas into singles wards, in order to create an environment where young men and women can find marriage partners.[10]

Third, LDS families are larger than the norm. Active Latter-day Saint families average 3.5 children compared to 2.75 children per family for inactive Latter-day Saints. By comparison, Protestants classified as "high-attending" had just over two children per family.[11] The trend to larger families still holds true though the numbers have been higher in previous generations. The high birthrate is fueled by their understanding that spirit children of God are waiting in the preexistence to gain bodies to enter this world.

The use of contraceptives has historically been frowned on by the LDS Church, although in recent years, the Church has chosen to enforce the ideal "in a positive, non-coercive manner."[12] Latter-day Saints are as likely to use modern birth control methods as the rest of the nation but less frequently and often not until after child-rearing has been completed.[13]

Fourth, LDS families are marked by more male authority and a traditional division of labor between husbands and wives. The stereotypical LDS mother — often referred to as "Molly Mormon" — doesn't work outside the home, cooks dinner every night, plans the family's camps and vacations, plays with her younger children and chauffeurs her older ones (in a minivan), cleans her own house, cans vegetables grown in the backyard, scrapbooks the family's history, sews quilts, arranges her own flowers, attends every additional meeting of the Relief Society, bakes homemade treats for her neighbors, and brings meals to the pregnant and elderly.[14]

Most LDS women find marriage and motherhood to be their most significant and desirable role. While the majority of married women remain at home when their children are young, many cultivate careers before and after that time.[15] The Church discourages women from taking employment while children are still at home, but they have not prohibited it outright for fear of placing members in conflict between "following the prophet" and meeting the economic needs of their family. Instead, Church leaders have stressed positive family practices and praised women for their virtue and strength.[16]

TENSIONS

The LDS Church faces certain tensions as family life in America changes. The ideal family conception championed within Mormonism places pressure on people who are not in traditional families, such as single mothers.[17] America has more adults choosing to live singly than ever. The average age of marriage is increasing. Women's roles are under pressure. The rise of feminism, coupled with economic necessity and changing standards of living, creates a higher expectation of meaningful employment. LDS women expect to become educated beyond merely what serves the home while some are calling for a higher profile for "Heavenly Mother" in LDS teaching. The most radical expression of changing attitudes among women is the desire among some to have more influence in governing the Church and even to gain a share in priesthood authority.

One area of family-related tension in the LDS Church comes from a vocal homosexual minority within Mormonism. Even though homosexuality is contrary to the LDS vision for families, a number of gay men and women value their LDS cultural heritage and identity and want to remain in relationship with their "people." Some are hoping that same-sex unions could be legitimized by the LDS Church in some way.[18]

In response to perceived threats to the family, the Church has occasionally felt a need to enter the political arena. Mormons care a great deal about defending the family against corrosive moral influences.[19] Church leaders mobilized LDS women to oppose the Equal Rights Amendment in the early 1970s and helped members organize against same-sex civil unions and legalized gambling in the 1990s.[20] These activities are seen as vices that undermine the sanctity and vitality of families.[21]

FAMILY PRACTICES

In the family the father is the priesthood leader. He uses his priesthood to bless and name his children when they are born and to baptize and confirm them at age eight. He will lay hands on the head of family members to give a blessing for health when they are sick, for comfort in times of tragedy, or for guidance when they face important decisions. He acts as a spiritual leader and counselor for the family.[22] Since the priesthood authority in a patriarchal family structure can be misused, the Church has spoken out strongly against spousal abuse.

Mormonism has no strong tradition of formal religious rituals in the home. They have no unique particular Sabbath rites, ceremonial meals, or special holiday practices. Religious ritual is found in Sacrament Meetings or the temple, not in the home setting. Mormon spirituality in the home is informal. Families engage in prayer and scripture study. They eat meals together frequently and say spontaneous prayers before meals. Sunday has a rhythm built around ward attendance, which often

AT A FAMILY GATHERING, PRIESTHOOD HOLDERS ORDAIN A TEENAGE BOY TO THE AARONIC PRIESTHOOD. © Jere Keys. Used by permission via Creative Commons.

includes a main meal after church services, with snacks and games in the evening.[23]

The most prominent expression of the family's spiritual life together is Family Home Evening. No church activities are organized on Monday nights and families clear their schedules for one or two hours of time together. The Church provides a lesson manual with teaching aids and suggested activities.[24] Family Home Evening is a time when families coordinate their event and transportation schedules for the week, discuss problems, pray, play games, plan service projects, or do fun outings together. Members of the family typically take turns to plan, lead music, teach the lesson, or prepare snacks.[25]

Reunions are common among Latter-day Saints. Keeping in touch with extended relatives is consistent with the belief in eternal families.[26] Some families maintain websites or newsletters while others create formal family organizations, complete with written values and mission statements.

Homes are decorated with objects that remind the family members of their values and commitments, or crafts made at home in the LDS tradition. Many families display a copy of an important statement from the General Authorities called "The Family: A Proclamation to the World,"[27] which summarizes the LDS view of family life. Such objects reinforce in the home environment important practices that take place in the chapel and the temple.[28]

POLYGAMY

At one time, plural marriage was an integral part of the fabric of LDS family life. Many Americans find this confusing and equate the Church of Jesus Christ of Latter-day Saints to the polygamous groups still operating throughout the American West.

Plural marriage was introduced by Joseph Smith, as outlined in Section 132 of the Doctrine and Covenants. It was practiced in secret by Mormon leaders for over a decade before it was openly avowed in 1852. An estimated 20 to 25 percent of Utah households were involved in polygamy during the decades between 1850 and 1890. As the United States government increased the pressure on the Mormons to end polygamy, at one point the existence of the Church was at stake. The prophet at that time, Wilford Woodruff, issued a statement (known as "The Manifesto") declaring that the Church would obey the law of the land, effectively ending the practice of plural marriage. Many leaders still lived with multiple wives after that time, and some continued to officiate over new polygamous unions until 1904, when plural marriage was firmly prohibited and those who advocated for it were disciplined.[29]

Splinter groups broke off from mainstream Mormonism, claiming that the mother church compromised under political pressure and wrongly abandoned a divinely revealed principle. Such groups are called "fundamentalists" because of their insistence on following Joseph Smith's teaching on marriage. The LDS Church repudiates the

THE BEEHIVE HOUSE IN SALT LAKE CITY WAS HOME TO MANY OF BRIGHAM YOUNG'S PLURAL WIVES. © Ross Anderson.

fundamentalist groups and excommunicates any members found to be practicing plural marriage.[30]

Yet, Mormons honor their pioneer forebears who lived in polygamy. Huge clans resulting from previous generations of polygamy still dominate the Church's top level leadership. Polygamy will forever be bound up in the social and cultural history of Mormonism.[31] While the LDS Church shuns any association with contemporary polygamy, plural marriage is still embraced as an eternal practice. Celestial families may include more than one wife. A number of contemporary LDS leaders are sealed to more than one woman for eternity, including former prophet Howard Hunter, who served as Church President until 1995.[32]

INTERACTING WITH YOUR NEIGHBOR

When it comes to family values, traditional Christians have a lot in common with Latter-day Saints. You can be allies with Mormons to speak up for the care and protection of families in your communities. Parents can share information and stories about child-rearing to build a rapport with your neighbor. After all, parents share common concerns and experiences regardless of divergent religious beliefs. If you are interested in genealogy or family history, your LDS neighbor can be a great source of insight, and this may also provide common ground.

We cannot accept the family as the basic unit of salvation or the idea of further extending our families for eternity. Families can be wonderful, but they aren't forever. Jesus taught that people will not be married in the next life (Matthew 22:30). We cannot assume that the life to come is merely a glorified version of the best elements of this life. The biblical vision of eternity is not marriage to our current spouse but marriage to Jesus Christ. The church collectively is referred to as his bride (Revelation 19:7 – 8). The intimate relationship we anticipate in eternity is with Jesus Christ and our Heavenly Father. Our joy is that God has made us a part of his forever family.

6

SACRED SPACE

L IFE IN THE local ward is not radically different from mainstream Christian congregations. Home life is similar as well. But there is no analogy to the LDS temple experience. The temple is the place where the unique elements of the underlying LDS worldview are most clearly expressed.

The LDS Church is aggressively building more temples. Temples typically rise as the LDS population in an area increases, allowing the Saints to have easier access to the ordinances vital to their exaltation. In 1975, the Church had sixteen temples. By 2000, there were 100, including temples in most medium-sized U.S. cities, including Boston, Dallas, San Diego, Baton Rouge, Las Vegas, and more.[1] At the end of 2010, 134 temples were in operation with seven more under construction.[2]

Mormons believe their temple ceremonies are the same as those performed in ancient temples.[3] The

THE SALT LAKE CITY TEMPLE.
© Ross Anderson.

temple provides a tangible representation of the holiness of God. It serves as a moral refuge, set apart from the evil and sensuality of the surrounding world, where the Saints engage most fully in the covenants and vows they have made toward God. Temple participation is reserved for those members who are living worthy lives.[4]

THE TEMPLE AND THE WARD

The local LDS ward is a public meeting place where a congregation lives out its common life. By contrast, the temple is private. It is not used for public worship. It is a place where only the most worthy can attend and experience divine presence in a distinctive way. The focus of the chapel is earthly living, where the ward bustles with noisy activity. The focus of the temple is eternity, where ceremonies are serene and hushed. In the local ward, people receive instruction about how to live worthy lives in this world. In the temple, faithful Saints are taught the secrets required to be exalted in the world to come.[5]

Latter-day Saints emphasize that what happens in the temple is "sacred, not secret." Mormons do not discuss the ordinances, even among themselves, outside the temple's walls because the ceremonies are considered too holy for speech. Access to the temple is limited. A member must be interviewed by the ward bishop to receive a "temple recommend," a card granting admission, as it were, into another realm.[6] The bishop discerns the applicant's worthiness by asking personal questions about such issues as loyalty to Church authorities, honesty, tithing, chastity, and family relationships. For those who have not attended before, the temple introduces a new dimension to their Mormon experience.[7]

No statistics are available to indicate what percentage of Latter-day Saints have temple recommends, but informal estimates suggest a minority of members are temple worthy, and even less attend the temple regularly. The temple recommend and the distinctive temple experience separate the Saints into two groups, creating a "church within a church."[8] Temple-goers are deeply involved and dedicated to the highest Mormon ideals. For new converts and those who choose not to pursue a temple recommend, Mormonism ends at the local meeting house.[9]

INSIDE THE TEMPLE

Each temple is designed to create a sense of connection to a sacred world beyond this earth. The temple stands in vivid contrast with the informality and lack of ceremony of the LDS Sunday services. Marked by excellent craftsmanship, the outside architecture sweeps the eye and mind in a vertical direction. Inside, the temple is divided into ceremonial rooms used for marriages, baptisms, and group instructional sessions.[10] Patrons change into simple white clothing upon arrival, symbolic of purity. Part of the temple clothing includes a holy undergarment designed to be worn daily outside the temple as a reminder of the covenants made in the temple.[11] Because of their sacred nature, these garments are not discussed or revealed publicly.[12]

Former Mormons talk about finding the temple ceremony — called "the endowment" — disturbing and unsettling. Active Saints may suppress similar feelings because of the importance and expectations attached to the endowment. Yet, many Latter-day Saints report special spiritual experiences in the temple, including a sense of peace and purposefulness. After all, they have left the ordinary world behind, prepared themselves to be worthy, adopted different clothing, and been initiated into mysteries of another realm. In some cases, temple patrons sense the presence of deceased ancestors, especially when performing proxy rites on their forefathers' behalf.[13]

At the end of the endowment ceremony, patrons gather in the Celestial Room, representing the highest heaven that dedicated Saints hope to achieve. In the Celestial Room, there are no images of clouds, angels, saints, deity, or any other traditional symbols of heaven. The room is basically a family sitting room where patrons can review what they have experienced. The celestial level of heaven is thus depicted as a place where the family gathers and is united in a divine state.[14]

THE TEMPLE AND ETERNAL FAMILIES

Temple ceremonies reinforce Mormonism's family-centered theology. The LDS vision of eternity posits families growing toward exaltation together. Becoming a god involves the power to extend one's family throughout eternity. The temple is an essential part of realizing this vision. Only marriages performed in the temple can endure beyond the grave,[15] thus binding children and parents, wives and husbands, to one another across generations and throughout time.[16]

The goal of active LDS parents is to see their children married in the temple so that as their children are sealed eternally to them, their grandchildren can likewise be sealed to their children, and so

TEMPLE SQUARE IN SALT LAKE CITY TEEMS WITH WEDDING PARTIES ON MOST WEEKENDS OF THE YEAR. © Ross Anderson.

on throughout infinite generations. Marriages that are performed for "time" only can later be upgraded to eternal marriages in the temple, while children born into temporal marriages can later be eternally sealed to their parents in the same way.

Ancestors who have died can also be united to the family in eternity by performing the necessary ordinances on their behalf. Active Latter-day Saints go to the temple to perform proxy baptisms, endowments, and marriage sealings for dead relatives, ordinances that are required for celestial exaltation and must be performed by someone holding priesthood authority. Mormons accept the responsibility for baptizing and sealing the marriages of those people who never had an opportunity to do this while alive,[17] which is the impulse behind the LDS interest in genealogy.

Birth and marriage records are submitted to the temples, and temple patrons perform the ceremonies vicariously in the names of deceased people.[18] Those who have been initiated into the endowment can go through the endowment for the dead. Teens are given special, limited access to the temple in order to perform proxy baptisms. While rites can be performed for anyone whose name has been discovered and filed, the major emphasis is on finding and doing the ordinances for one's own family.

INTERACTING WITH YOUR NEIGHBOR

Traditional Christianity does not view temples the way Mormonism does. Latter-day Saints claim that their temple ceremonies are the same today as they were in ancient Israel. Yet, nothing in the biblical description of the temple ritual suggests the kind of ordinances Mormons practice. The biblical temple was the site of animal sacrifices. It was patterned after the tabernacle in Exodus, which consisted only of a courtyard and two rooms (Hebrews 9:2 – 5). The permanent temple added some storerooms, but the basic layout remained the same. The biblical record does not indicate marriages were performed there and speaks of nothing remotely similar to the endowment ceremony.

Furthermore, no animal sacrifices are carried out in LDS temples as they were in ancient times. In fact, according to Hebrews 8 – 10, the one final sacrifice on the cross rendered the work done in ancient temples obsolete. Thus, as Ephesians 2:19 – 22 says, the physical temple has been replaced by something new. The people of God are now "a holy temple in the Lord … in which God lives by his Spirit." Because God dwells collectively in his people, his presence is no longer mediated by special sacred space. In other words, physical temples no longer have a place in God's plan.

Your LDS friend will probably hesitate to talk much about the temple — especially about what happens within it, as it is not a topic for idle or curious conversation. If you live in an area where an LDS temple is opening, go on a temple tour with your neighbor. Before temples are dedicated, they are open to the public. It provides a rare opportunity to talk to your friend about what the temple means.

Christians don't believe that the temple ceremonies are from God, but there is no need to mock what others find sacred. Because the temple is viewed as sacred, Saints will be offended when anything associated with the temple is treated lightly or derided, such as when a website posts photos of people in temple garments or publishes the text of the temple ritual. Street preachers have made a scene in front of an LDS temple by waving a temple garment over their heads while denouncing Latter-day Saint beliefs. This kind of behavior has an intense emotional effect.

In Acts 19, the apostle Paul experienced powerful results from his preaching, to the degree that the craftsmen who made idols feared for their livelihood since so many people were turning to follow Jesus. In Paul's defense, one of the leading citizens of the city testified that Paul and his companions had never blasphemed the city's goddess (Acts 19:37). It is possible to bear witness for Jesus without tearing down what others revere. The people of Ephesus did not come to Christ because Paul ridiculed their goddess but because they observed the power of Jesus Christ.

Keep in mind that you can expect to have different kinds of conversations between "temple Mormons" and those who have not been endowed. The two groups will likely have very different experiences with and attitudes about the LDS Church. Yet, be aware that even less active Mormons will be offended if things held to be sacred in their culture are mocked.

7

LATTER-DAY SAINT PIETY

M ORMONISM IS MORE than a belief system. It is a cultural identity that gives rise to a particular way of life. Latter-day Saints act out such a lifestyle in relation to the Church as a whole, the local ward, the family, and the temple. The lifestyle also takes shape in a commitment to personal spiritual practices such as prayer, scripture study, service, chastity, fasting, tithing, and dietary restrictions.[1]

CONVERSION COMES FIRST

The spiritual life of individual Mormons begins with a conversion experience, for those born into the faith and those who join it. Evangelicals think of conversion as the moment of being spiritually regenerated or "born again," when they acknowledge their sinful nature, trust in Christ for forgiveness, and discover a new way of life. For Latter-day Saints, conversion is the moment when they come to know with divinely-inspired certainty that Joseph Smith is a prophet, the Book of Mormon is true, and the LDS Church is the only true church.[2] The Saints are taught to seek this "testimony" of the truth by sincere prayer, expecting that God will make the truth known to them through what most describe as a warm, positive feeling or a "still, small voice" of divine inspiration.[3]

THE IMPULSE TO ACHIEVE

The LDS worldview is defined by the principle of progression toward exaltation that works out in LDS life as a drive for achievement or advancement. Titles in the LDS hymnbook suggest this: "I Have Work Enough to Do," "Keep the Commandments," "Let Us All Press on in the Work of the Lord," and "Put Your Shoulder to the Wheel." This last hymn urges its singers to "push every worthy work along" by reminding them that "we all have work, let no one shirk."[4]

Latter-day Saints have a "can-do" attitude that emphasizes intellectual growth.[5] The Church praises knowledge and learning, based on the principle that "the glory of God is intelligence."[6] Mormons see education as a sacred charge. Joseph Smith instructed the Saints to "seek ye out of the best books words of wisdom; seek learning, even by study and also by faith," and to study all people and nations, near and far.[7] This explains why Latter-day Saints generally have high achievement rates in education, including higher rates of high school graduation, college graduation, and doctoral degrees than other Americans.[8]

The drive to achieve is also expressed economically. LDS leaders portray money as positive rather than dangerous, so Mormons are comfortable with success and wealth. Many of the Church's General Authorities were successful businessmen and entrepreneurs. There is no ascetic tradition in Mormonism, and affluence is typically perceived as a sign of God's blessing.[9]

Latter-day Saints are taught to provide for their own material wellbeing through hard work and prudent living. Birthed in part by the need to survive in an inhospitable land, the pervasive Mormon work ethic posits that "each laborer shall be worthy of his hire and that no one deserves a financial reward if he or she has not earned it."[10] Along with getting an education, working hard, and avoiding debt, the Church teaches members to store away an emergency supply of food and other basic necessities.[11] The Church encourages its members "to prepare for adversity in life by having a basic supply of food and water and some money in savings," including staples to last up to two years, and a three-month "supply of food that is part of your normal, daily diet."[12]

Anonymous. Used by permission via Creative Commons.

Besides financial and educational achievement, Latter-day Saints are expected to work hard to cultivate a lifestyle of personal righteousness. Mormons often speak of this in terms of "worthiness," the single most compelling motive driving daily life in the LDS culture.[13] Speaking of the priesthood, a recent LDS prophet declared, "Personal worthiness becomes the standard of eligibility to receive and exercise this sacred power."[14] Worthiness is generated by obedience. Children are to obey their parents. At baptism, members make a covenant to keep God's commandments.[15] Members of the ward are to obey their leaders and to "magnify their callings." The Saints are often exhorted to "follow the prophet." Temple patrons make solemn vows and promises.[16]

WORTHY LIVING

Worthiness is expressed by living up to the Church's standards, starting with modest dress and conservative grooming. Church standards include honesty, purity (including avoiding immoral movies and vulgar language), and chastity.[17] Members are held accountable to these standards through regular worthiness interviews by ward officials.

Tithing is another practice among worthy Latter-day Saints. The LDS Church teaches that giving ten percent of one's income to the Church is a commandment of God. Tithe-paying is required to be considered worthy of access to the temple. The bishop interviews individual members annually to find out if they have paid their entire tithing obligation.[18]

Worthy Latter-day Saints give a tremendous amount of time and energy in service, not only fulfilling their primary ward callings, but working on welfare farms, doing genealogy and temple work for ancestors, baking casseroles for neighbors, helping the needy in their community, and more.

Two distinct expressions of LDS personal righteousness that attract a lot of attention are the "Word of Wisdom" and the "Law of Chastity." The "Law of Chastity" dictates that any sexual relations or practices outside of traditional marriage are forbidden.[19] The Church stresses that adultery is second in seriousness only to murder. Leaders strongly emphasize the dangers of sexual sin, especially to young members. Moral purity is a major focus of the bishop's worthiness interviews with teens. Young people are instructed not to date before age sixteen, to go out mainly in groups, and to date only those with high standards. When sexual transgressions do occur, full forgiveness requires confession to Church authorities and a process of church discipline.[20]

The Word of Wisdom is a unique health code outlined in Section 89 of the Doctrine and Covenants, which forbids alcohol, tobacco, coffee, and tea. Some Saints understand it to apply to caffeine in any form, including soft drinks.[21] Inactive members typically don't take the Word of Wisdom too seriously, but active members demonstrate a striking difference from normal American practices.[22] Instead of alcohol or tobacco, many Mormons indulge in sugar. A number of LDS cultural traditions revolve around some form of sweets.[23] Mormons consume more Jell-O, ice cream, marshmallows, and chocolate chips than other Americans.[24]

PERSONAL SPIRITUALITY

LDS personal piety is not just about living up to a sufficient level of righteousness to be counted worthy. Rather, it is cultivated by a variety of personal spiritual practices, including scripture reading and prayer. Latter-day Saints are regularly challenged by their leaders to read through the Book of Mormon. Three-quarters of Mormons say they read the scriptures privately at least once a week, compared to 35 percent of the general population. Eight of ten pray daily.[25] LDS prayer is unrehearsed and spontaneous, except for a few prescribed prayers associated with certain ordinances. Mormons address God most commonly as "Heavenly Father" and end each prayer with the phrase "in the name of Jesus Christ, amen."[26] In contrast to the familiarity and intimacy with God often expressed by evangelicals in prayer, Latter-day Saints pray in the formal "thee" and "thou" language of the King James Bible as a sign of reverence toward God.

LATTER-DAY SAINTS ARE DEVOTED TO STUDYING THE BOOK OF MORMON. © Stephanie Hawver. Used by permission via Creative Commons.

Saints couple their spiritual devotions with journaling. While not seen as a requirement, keeping a journal is strongly recommended as a way of preserving one's personal history for future generations.[27]

Active Mormons honor the Sabbath day by not working unless absolutely necessary, and by reserving Sundays for church attendance and family time. Eating out, going to the mall or the movies, buying gas, doing grocery shopping, and similar activities are discouraged because they require others to work on Sunday.[28] The power of this conviction is illustrated in Utah whenever the Fourth of July falls on a Sunday, as many towns reschedule their patriotic celebrations for Saturday night.

The first Sunday of every month is set aside for Latter-day Saints to fast. Many Saints also fast and pray privately for guidance or to address special concerns.[29]

SPIRITUAL EXPERIENCES

Latter-day Saints often report having personal spiritual experiences where they "feel the Spirit." These experiences involve tender emotions, which are understood to be the activity of the Spirit of God bearing witness of the truth.[30] These emotionally moving events may come in conjunction with a priesthood blessing or in times when God's help is earnestly sought. While deeply emotional, these spiritual encounters are marked more by orderly reflection than enthusiastic expression.[31] In the evangelical world, spiritual encounters may happen in group settings, stirred up by dynamic worship or a powerful speaker. For Mormons, these sacred experiences happen more often in private settings and are not widely shared with others.

Latter-day Saints often experience this sense of the Spirit when seeking God's guidance. Saints believe that the LDS Church is guided by revelation through its highest leaders, but members also expect to receive divine revelation for their own lives: for direction in their work or ministry calling, for wisdom to solve family problems, or for guidance in career or marriage decisions.[32] Inspiration comes in the form of a warm or peaceful feeling, or a sense of insight or clarity about a particular decision. It can also come through the words of a priesthood blessing or the prayers of another member.

INTERACTING WITH YOUR NEIGHBOR

Latter-day Saints practice many of the same moral virtues and spiritual disciplines as traditional Christians, which can provide some common ground for discussion as the relationship with your neighbor grows. You can share what you are reading and learning in your Bible study, or how God is leading you through prayer. Simply share your own experience while listening to your neighbor's experiences, praying the door will open to Christ-centered and biblically informed conversation. In this way, you can avoid the discussion becoming an argument or doctrinal battle.

Because Latter-day Saints take obedience and righteous living seriously, Mormons have a major issue with traditional Christianity. Too many Latter-day Saints can recount stories of people they know who profess saving faith in Christ but who don't live chaste, honest, or self-controlled lives. Mormons often conclude that the Christian gospel is empty and powerless. When I shared the message of God's grace with one LDS man, he told me about his brother who professes to be an evangelical Christian but who is living in adultery. To him, the Christian message sounds like nothing more than, "Just pray a prayer to 'accept Jesus' and you'll get into heaven, even though you keep on living like hell." This perception is a serious obstacle to our faith-sharing. We need to live our lives in a way that supports the credibility of our message.

Our righteous lifestyle is not motivated by the attempt to become worthy of the celestial kingdom. The Bible teaches us to live righteous lives as a response to being redeemed by the infinite grace of God (Titus 2:11 – 14). God's grace gives us tremendous freedom, not to live a life of sin, but to be loved and accepted unconditionally even when we can't live up to God's perfect standards.

The message of unconditional grace can speak powerfully to Latter-day Saints, especially when it comes from a person whose life has moral integrity. It's the message they need to hear. Many devoted members feel they can never measure up to the standards set by the Church. The quest for increasing worthiness can leave average Saints weary and disheartened.[33] How do you know if your efforts are good enough or when you've done enough?

This can take a toll on conscientious members. A study released in March 2008 by a federal agency found that Utah, which is 60 percent

Mormon, has the highest rate of adults who report feeling "serious psychological distress." Utahans also have the highest use of anti-depressants in the nation. Of course, statistics can be interpreted in different ways.[34] One Utah psychiatrist relates these findings to the extraordinary expectations of achievement and worthiness placed on Latter-day Saints, especially women, which drive them to maintain a constant image of perfection.[35]

A number of LDS scholars are appealing for a greater emphasis on grace in Mormonism. One respected LDS scholar writes: "It is lamentably ironic how grace can be edged out of Mormon theology," which results in "a religious culture where the status of grace is uncertain."[36] LDS scripture passages are being reinterpreted by some to make more room for the concept of grace.[37] Whether the Church's leadership will follow this trend is unknown. Nonetheless, this may signal an increasing responsiveness among Latter-day Saints to the biblical message of God's unconditional grace.

When Saints come to feel defeated in their pursuit of worthiness, they have four options. They can try harder. They can pretend to try harder, in order to maintain the public image of worthiness. They can reinterpret the standards downward so that they feel as if they are measuring up. Or they can just give up. When our LDS friends come to sense the futility of their efforts, a kind, trusted Christian friend can provide a safe listening ear.

In the end, our message to Latter-day Saints is that there is a different way. Hope lies in adopting a completely different approach to God, not in trying harder to achieve the impossible. Our confidence in God is not based on merit but on mercy. One of the greatest gifts we can offer our LDS neighbors is an invitation to discover how they can experience God's unconditional grace through Jesus Christ.

Just remember, when you do have a chance to talk to your LDS friends, you probably don't want to offer them a cup of coffee. But cookies or ice cream will be welcome!

8

US AND THEM

L ATTER-DAY SAINTS SEE the world through the lens of their own identity and experience. Other people are either Mormons, potential converts to Mormonism, ex-Mormons, or anti-Mormons. Church leaders encourage the Saints to interact with nonmembers in an effort to overcome clannishness,[1] but members continue to address each other in the language of insiders. Calling each other "brother" and "sister," for example, reminds everyone of who is included and who is excluded.[2]

The confidence of the Latter-day Saints that theirs is the only true church creates an impression to outsiders of arrogance.[3] One LDS scholar identifies how this attitude is expressed in folk humor.

Out of this belief is often born a smug self-righteousness that is evident in jokes Mormons tell about their dealings with people of other faiths. For example, when a public school teacher asked a little Mormon boy in her class what he would be if he weren't Mormon, he replied, 'Embarrassed.'"

But the Saints have another body of humor in which they poke fun at themselves and their exclusivity.[4] (Of course, such jokes and the attitude they betray are not exclusive to Mormonism.)

ACCOMMODATING THE OUTSIDE WORLD

In the early years of Mormonism, many factors — theology, polygamy, and geographical isolation among others — contributed to a sense of Latter-day Saints being different from the rest of America. Since the end of polygamy in 1890, Mormons have hungered for acceptance in the larger society. They have emphasized their patriotism and welcomed every favorable mention in the national press. The Church began to deemphasize doctrine and draw attention to the strengths and virtues of Mormon culture. Particularly in the 1950s, the LDS focus on traditional values and strong families cast the Mormons as ideal American citizens.[5]

A tension has always been present in Mormonism between the things unique to it and the things in common with American culture. When the unique elements — such as Mormonism's additional scripture and prophetic claims — become more prominent, the pre-

MISSIONARY TOUR GUIDES AND MUSEUM-LIKE DISPLAYS AT TEMPLE SQUARE IN SALT LAKE CITY PROMOTE LDS CLAIMS TO THOUSANDS OF VISITORS EACH YEAR. © Ross Anderson.

vailing relationship between Mormonism and America is antagonism. When more emphasis is placed on the common elements, the relationship is assimilation.[6] The tug-of-war between cultural relevance (assimilation) versus social and theological uniqueness (antagonism) is reflected in products marketed to LDS consumers. T-shirts and toys may communicate central Book of Mormon themes, but they do so by copycatting the look and style of popular brand names.[7]

Sociologists theorize that any church succeeds by remaining different, but not too different; this pattern thus establishes a medium level of tension with the surrounding society. The LDS Church has periodically acted to keep this tension from becoming too extreme, such as the 1978 revelation that granted the priesthood to males of all races.[8] Mormonism appeared to be moving toward antagonism in the mid-twentieth century with a renewed emphasis on the Book of Mormon, missionary work, genealogy, and temple construction, along with a movement to centralize and standardize church programs. Recently, the pendulum has swung back toward assimilation, as certain traditional doctrines and writings have been downplayed.[9]

The traditional values that placed Mormonism in the mainstream fifty years ago are no longer as prevalent in American society as a whole. Mormonism's clean-cut image and family values may be moving the LDS Church farther out of step with the mainstream, creating a new form of antagonism. Since the public is still uncomfortable with some elements of Mormon theology and culture, the LDS Church has developed a way of speaking in carefully crafted language to convey different messages to insiders versus outsiders,[10] often called the "milk before meat" approach. The premise is that people are not ready to digest deeper doctrines and esoteric practices until they have had a chance to adopt simpler, more appealing concepts.[11] It often comes across as dishonest, because a potential convert is asked to make a serious life commitment when some relevant information has been knowingly withheld.

GAINING CONVERTS

The LDS Church works hard to maintain a positive public image, in part to attract potential converts. In the mid-twentieth century, the Church organized a public relations office in Utah, then hired a New York public relations firm in the 1990s. Its family-oriented television and radio ads, along with the Tabernacle Choir, the welfare and humanitarian programs, Brigham Young University athletics, and the success stories of LDS celebrities all intentionally show Mormons at their best. In this way they create a more attractive image of the Church.[12] In 2010, an ad campaign hit TV screens in several American cities, "making the case that some of the coolest and most hip people in the world are Mormons."

"I'm a surfer, a woman and a woman's longboard champion, and I'm a Mormon," says one of the ads, featuring Hawaiian pro surfer Joy Monahan. Another ad features artist Cassandra Barney, who says, "I am an artist and the mother of three beautiful girls, and I am a Mormon."

An LDS spokesman commented that "our effort is really to try to help people understand that Mormons are not as different as you would think."[13]

LDS MISSIONARIES ARE ACTIVELY SEEKING CONVERTS IN OVER 80 COUNTRIES AROUND THE WORLD. © Ragne Kabanova. Shutterstock.com. Used by permission.

Ultimately, the Church's carefully crafted public image is related to its stated purpose of proclaiming the Mormon message. Mormonism has always been driven by a strong impulse to convert others. In 2010, the LDS Church fielded over 50,000 volunteer missionaries in 344 different regions covering almost every nation of the world, resulting in about a million new members being added worldwide every three years.[14]

LDS boys are taught from a young age that their obligation is to serve a mission when they turn nineteen. Missionaries go where they are sent by the Church and their families pay their expenses for a two-year mission term. They live cheaply, isolated from home life and from worldly attractions. They can't dance or listen to popular music, read magazines, or go to movies. No romantic relationships are allowed. They work six long days per week, passing out literature, knocking on doors, and speaking on street corners to share the Mormon message. A mission is not considered a duty for young women but many do serve in the same way as young men. (Women make up about 20 percent of the LDS missionary force.)[15] Several thousands of retirees also go on missions. Older missionaries provide leadership, work with public relations, serve in genealogy libraries and temples, teach classes, and much more.[16]

Serving a mission is a rite of passage that strengthen's young people's LDS identity and establishes their faithfulness. The mission functions as a training ground for the next generation of Mormon leaders.[17] My neighbor speaks with great pride about her son on a mission. A returned missionary is incorporated back into Mormon society with new status, rights, and responsibilities, ready for a more mature level of commitment to the Church.[18]

Church members also take responsibility for missionary outreach, in partnership with the missionaries. They are taught to see themselves as "member missionaries," which entails building relationships with friends or neighbors in the hope that interested prospects will take the missionary lessons. When missionaries generate contacts by cold calling, one in one thousand joins the Church. By contrast, when they meet by appointment with an interested person in the home of a Latter-day Saint friend or relative, conversion occurs 50 percent of the time.[19]

MORMONISM AND TRADITIONAL CHRISTIANITY

Mormonism has been at odds with historic biblical Christianity from its inception. The LDS claim of being the restored church is also an indictment of traditional Christianity. Joseph Smith alleged that God told him to join no church because all of the existing churches and their beliefs were wrong, abominable, and corrupt.[20] The LDS Church has softened its public stance about other churches in recent years, but the attitude expressed in Joseph Smith's statements is still commonly held.

Yet, common ground exists between traditional Christians and Latter-day Saints. In order to advance unique truth claims, Mormonism had to emphasize the points of divergence. The Bible was not abandoned but other sacred texts were adopted along with it. Baptism was retained but the meaning was reinterpreted, with the addition of baptism for the dead. The Lord's Supper was maintained as a memorial act, in the form of the sacrament service, but water replaced wine. Mormonism retained Christian hymnody and sacred music, but developed their own hymns with distinctly Mormon content. Trinitarianism was replaced with a doctrine of three distinct beings who form one godhead — but not one God. The doctrine of the preexistence was introduced. Above all, traditional biblical beliefs about the afterlife were replaced with the concept of eternal, exalted families.[21]

Mormons believe that only they have the authority to act for God and that only ordinances performed by that authority are valid in eternity. While members of other churches may achieve a level of heaven, they cannot be exalted to the highest level without embracing Mormonism.[22] At the same time, Mormons want to be accepted as legitimate

Christians who belong to a bona fide Christian church. This creates a dilemma. Latter-day Saints want to claim exclusivity, yet "are chagrined when they are excluded from the very community of believers they have just excoriated."[23] Latter-day Saints can't seem to see the contradiction inherent in wanting to be accepted as another Christian body while aggressively trying to convert members of Christian churches.

LATTER-DAY SAINTS IN PUBLIC LIFE

The LDS Church and its members relate to the outside world in other ways beside missionary activity — although the missionary impulse is not far below the surface at any time. In recent years, the Church has stepped up its humanitarian activities around the world. Charitable assistance is given regardless of religion and is often distributed in cooperation with other faith-based charities.[24]

Latter-day Saints are active in the business world at every level, just as the LDS Church itself owns and manages a number of for-profit businesses. Mormon cultural values seem to be compatible with business success: Latter-day Saints tend to work hard, strive to achieve, and are ethical, frugal, and well-organized. Teens develop leadership skills in priesthood quorums and Scouting, while the mission experience trains young adults in the habits of discipline and perseverance.

Mormons tend to be actively involved in government and politics, locally and nationally. Joseph Smith revered the U.S. Constitution[25] and taught the Church to support the law and those who administer it.[26] Nearly two-thirds of Latter-day Saints identify with or lean toward the Republican Party. They also tend to take conservative positions on social and political issues like abortion, homosexuality, and the size and role of government.[27] Apparently, most Mormons believe that LDS doctrines and practices are not consistent with a liberal political philosophy. They generally see labor unions and government social programs — both traditionally related to the Democratic

Party — as circumventing the work ethic. The LDS Church occasionally involves itself in political controversies but only on moral issues, where the Church feels a responsibility to act.[28]

The Church has found itself embroiled in controversy in recent years in its relationship with the community. Jewish groups have expressed alarm over proxy baptisms performed for victims of the Holocaust.[29] Fears were voiced during Mitt Romney's presidential run that the Church might exercise undue influence over members elected to public office.[30] The Church received a violent backlash after its prominent involvement in the passing of California's Proposition 8 banning same-sex marriages.[31]

The history of violent action against the Saints in the nineteenth century has created a sort of persecution complex. Mormons can be hypersensitive about criticism. Regardless of their motivation or tone, those who publicly disagree with LDS claims are often summarily labeled "anti-Mormon." Yet, some materials published by Christian ministries are inaccurate and inflammatory. I've already mentioned what happened in California after Proposition 8 passed, and the response to Mitt

DEMONSTRATORS GATHERED AT THE LDS LOS ANGELES TEMPLE TO PROTEST THE CHURCH'S STAND AGAINST HOMOSEXUAL MARRIAGE. © John Nakamura Remy. Used by permission via Creative Commons.

Romney's candidacy often fell into what might be called "negative profiling."[32] My brother told me about how, after the Proposition 8 election, he and his friends were mocked and cursed at a college basketball game, simply because they were BYU fans. So while many Latter-day Saints are overly defensive, they also have some legitimate concerns.

INTERACTING WITH YOUR NEIGHBOR

Given their desire for positive recognition, your LDS friend will probably be delighted when you affirm something about Mormonism, though he may interpret any positive affirmation as another proof of the truth of Mormonism. We can be confident and mature enough to give credit where credit is due. We're not giving anything away if we acknowledge something good about Mormonism. Genuine recognition has a way of disarming the defensiveness that many Saints harbor.

As you develop a spiritual conversation with your neighbor, he or she may not seem interested in your perspective. I once offered to give a traditional Christian perspective to a local LDS Institute of Religion class on comparative faiths. The teacher wasn't interested. Latter-day Saints are content in their certainty and don't think other faiths have much to offer. Often, the only way they've ever been approached to talk about faith has been from an adversarial stance. You have an opportunity to break their stereotypes of traditional Christians by kindness and consideration.

Your LDS neighbor hopes to see you take an interest in investigating Mormonism. You may be asked to read the Book of Mormon. Your friend will believe that this is the most effective way to convert you, since the Book of Mormon itself promises that God will reveal the truth of it to anyone who will read and pray about it. I don't see any harm in reading the Book of Mormon if you evaluate it from a sound biblical perspective. In fact, this is a good way to engage your friend in conversation about spiritual truth. Encourage your neighbor to read it with you and answer your questions along the way. Invite him or her to read the New Testament and talk with you about it every few chapters.

You may also be invited to take the missionary lessons. A young friend of mine took up the offer as a way to learn more about how to share his faith with Latter-day Saints. Generally, I don't recommend this. You can evaluate the entire content of the missionary lessons online.[33] It doesn't make sense even to go down that road, since you will certainly be drawn into a debate. The missionaries will not be interested in continuing on those terms, and neither should you. Furthermore, if you are not well versed in LDS and biblical beliefs, you might become confused.

Your friend may be reticent to fully explain everything that Mormonism stands for, reasoning that you're not ready for the "meat" until you swallow the "milk." The Church has a website for the general public — www.mormon.org — where LDS doctrines are explained in only the most general terms, using terminology that sounds very much like traditional Christianity. Some of the essential but esoteric teachings of Mormonism are sidestepped. One page mentions the goal of "becoming like our Heavenly Father" but never defines that as becoming divine. Another entry mentions going to the celestial kingdom to be with worthy family members but never reveals what that entails or what happens there. Mormons are aware of how different their worldview is and how strange it can sound to nonmembers if not carefully couched.

Be careful how you phrase things since Mormons often expect criticism. Make your point or ask your question respectfully and gently, avoiding any kind of derogatory tone. If you're only trying to score points in a debate, your intent will quickly become obvious and will shut down communication and trust. Simply bringing up a question or difficult issue, even if done sensitively, can feel like a threat to your friend and send him or her backing away. Be patient. Don't push it. Keep reaching out in areas where you have common ground, knowing that many Latter-day Saints have eventually chosen to adopt the historic biblical Christian faith.

9

JOINING AND LEAVING

IN 2009, THE LDS Church reported almost 14 million members world-wide, compared to three million in 1971. The Church grows by bap-tizing converts and by the birth of children.[1] One-quarter of church members are converts to the faith. Half of these converts were raised Protestant, one-fourth were raised Catholic, and one-in-five were raised with no religious affiliation.[2] Due to declining birth rates, slower conversion rates, and poor retention of converts, growth has decreased from over 5 percent each year in the late 1980s to less than 2 percent in the mid – 2000s.[3] In 1989, the average LDS missionary baptized eight people into the Church. By 2004, the number dropped to 4.5. Only 1.2 of the 4.5 converts baptized each year by the typical missionary will remain active in the Church.[4]

The relationship of individuals with the Church can be seen as a continuum. On one end are the ardent apologists for the Church for whom Mormonism is a lens through which all reality is perceived and understood. On the other end are the apostates, who have left Mormonism and maintain no relationship with the Church or the LDS community. In between is a wide variety of experiences and lev-els of allegiance. At the center of the spectrum are those who hold a Mormon worldview, but also look at life through other frameworks derived from history, philosophy, science, social science, or literature.

Some of these rigidly divide alternative perspectives from their LDS worldview while others find ways to integrate them.[5]

Another way to think about the different ways Latter-day Saints relate to the Church is to compare two factors: identification and belief.[6] Some Saints identify strongly with LDS culture and community, others less strongly, while some come to reject the Mormon community entirely. Some Saints hold LDS beliefs strongly, others less strongly, while others have rejected the LDS belief system. This classification results in nine types of Latter-day Saints, from "fervent followers" to "apostates."

WHY PEOPLE JOIN

People join the LDS Church for a myriad of reasons. Many will cite the testimony experience they received while investigating Mormonism. For some, Mormonism provides answers they find satisfying about the meaning of life.[7] Some find the emphasis on righteousness and achievement appealing while others like the teaching that almost everyone goes to some form of heaven, or that there is a second chance for salvation after this life is over. Many people feel the LDS Church makes God understandable compared to the biblical doctrine of the Trinity.

LEVELS OF LDS BELIEF AND IDENTIFICATION

Fervent Followers. Accept LDS claims wholeheartedly and attend meetings, pay full tithes, hold temple recommends.

Ritualists. Fully involved in social activities but limited understanding or acceptance of basic tenets of the faith.

Cultural Saints. Identify with Mormon roots and ancestry but reject the unique doctrines and claims of the LDS church.

Outsiders. Retain beliefs in basic doctrines but maintain little or no involvement in the LDS community.

Marginal Saints. Low in both religious beliefs and community involvement. Passively disengaged from the church.

Doctrinal Apostates. Reject basic beliefs of the church and have actively distanced themselves from the LDS community.

Splinter Saints. Claim some of the distinctive LDS beliefs, but maintain no communal involvement whatsoever.

Social Apostates. Reject the LDS community and most LDS beliefs, but for mainly relational versus doctrinal reasons.

Apostates. Reject both beliefs and community identification. Generally devote energy to opposing the church.

For others, emotional reasons play a role in their decision to convert. The idea of eternal families is appealing, as is the idea of a second chance, especially for those who have lost a loved one. People also find security in the structure and authority of Mormonism. Some encounter the LDS Church when they are searching spiritually or looking to fill a void in their hearts while others find a welcoming, supportive community when going through tough times emotionally. The Church seems like a safe haven from the evils of society for troubled families.

Some join for relational reasons. Young people growing up in areas where Mormonism is in the majority may become members because of social pressure while others join through a romantic relationship with a Latter-day Saint. I've also known people who joined the LDS Church because, during a time of material need, LDS neighbors were helpful and supportive. Some join the Church to try to gain access to financial help.

Most Latter-day Saints were raised in Mormonism and became official Church members by baptism at age eight. The majority stay

CHILDREN ARE TYPICALLY BAPTIZED INTO MEMBERSHIP IN THE LDS CHURCH AT AGE EIGHT.
Anonymous. Used by permission via Creative Commons.

in the Church, although they may experience periods of increased or decreased activity. Whether it's the power of their testimony experience, the truth claims of the Church, or strong community relationships, Mormonism provides people a positive way of life and a caring society where people look out for each other. People like the activity and basic personal disciplines encouraged in Mormonism that give the sense that they are building something significant in this life and the next. All in all, Mormonism provides a comprehensive life experience, a many-faceted, ordered existence that encompasses all of life, in the face of the world's questions and sorrows.[8]

WHY PEOPLE LEAVE

In spite of these positive factors, people are leaving the LDS Church. The Church has not found a completely effective way of connecting new members to the Mormon community or helping them build a sense of LDS identity.[9] Up to 50 percent of converts in the United States drop out after a year.[10]

When it comes to lifelong members, Mormonism has a relatively high retention rate. Seven in ten of those raised Mormon still identify as Mormon in adulthood. Of those who do leave the faith, about half find a home in a new religion while the other half become unaffiliated with any faith.[11]

One study from 1983 that examined the reasons why people leave Mormonism found that 43 percent left due to unmet spiritual needs.[12] People leave Mormonism for a combination of many reasons — a process scholars call "deconversion." It may be that they don't want to live the LDS lifestyle anymore or want to live contrary to Church standards. Members tire of the stress of living up to the high expectations of activity and worthiness, the constant busyness, time pressures, and money pressures. People discover unsavory episodes in the Church's history that cast a negative light on Church's prophets or contradict official Church accounts. Often converts uncover some shocking information they were unaware of when they chose to be baptized, such as temple practices or the idea of becoming gods.

Honest questions go unanswered and discouragement comes when people are told not to question the faith. Some leave because they come to believe that LDS claims cannot stand up to rational or intellectual scrutiny while others decide that Mormon doctrines do not conform to the teachings of the Bible. Many leave because they simply don't fit in culturally. Some are poorly treated and don't come back. Just as many Latter-day Saints have their faith confirmed by warm spiritual experiences, some also leave because of an experience — a dream or spiritual feeling — that caused them to doubt Mormonism.

LEAVING IS DIFFICULT

Leaving Mormonism is not easy, especially for those raised LDS. They must swim against the tide of a strong group identity and deep cultural roots. When a person rejects the revelations and ordinances of Mormonism, he or she is considered apostate[13] — a label usually employed in an uncomplimentary sense. Latter-day Saints are taught to fear the prospect of apostasy. They are warned that to leave the Church is to walk out from under the safe umbrella of the priesthood's care and authority. LDS curriculum explains that members who leave do so because of pride, sin, or pettiness — or because they are deceived by Satan.[14] The Book of Mormon teaches that those who "depart from the truth" will be judged in the final judgment for falling prey to this deception.[15] This negative picture weighs heavily on those who might think about leaving.

Although many leave to be true to themselves or to embrace a new belief structure, they leave at a cost.[16] An ex-Mormon may suffer a sense of anguish over the loss of his or her identity,[17] including traditions, heritage, and stories. Family life and personal relationships are disrupted. The former Mormon may feel pressured by ward members or church officials and is likely to be shunned by friends and family.[18] Those who leave are often misunderstood, stereotyped, and slandered, under the assumption that people don't leave the Church unless they are uncommitted or have sinned.[19] Resigning from the Church is never seen by LDS peers as being a positive or enlightened choice.

As a result, a doubting Latter-day Saint may go through an agonizing transition period, perhaps years long, marked by insecurity, alienation, anger, and confusion. He or she may wrestle with feelings of guilt, denial, shame, and loneliness before ultimately accepting the decision to leave the Church.[20]

NEW ORDER MORMONS

In rejecting the claims and teachings of Mormonism, some nevertheless decide to stay in the Church as "closet doubters." They no longer believe the fundamental claims of the Church but continue to attend meetings and fulfill their ward callings, holding temple recommends, and serving in leadership roles.[21] Referred to as New Order Mormons, they "recognize both good and bad in the Church, and have determined that the Church does not have to be perfect in order to remain useful."[22]

Disaffected Mormons stay in the Church for a variety of reasons. Marriage to an active Saint compels some to stay to provide stability for the family. The prospect of divorce keeps others from leaving the Church, and some stay because of their family history and traditions. Job security is a real issue, especially in Utah, where the Church employs thousands of people, or where one's boss and coworkers may be LDS. Social life for many revolves around friends who are active Saints, and they stay because they have no idea where to go or what to do apart from Mormonism. By staying involved, some hope they can influence the Church to change while others see the Church as a safe community in which to raise their children with positive values.[23] Some stay because they still appreciate some, if not all, of the teachings and practices of the Church while others stay in spite of their unbelief.

INTERACTING WITH YOUR NEIGHBOR

If your LDS friend has doubts about Mormonism, it can be difficult to build enough trust for him or her to open up to you about it. Admitting such doubts puts your friend in a perilous place. They do not want to become an apostate and may have a great deal to lose. Don't push. Latter-day Saints have a lot of reasons not to change. I am acquainted with many former Mormons, and they are among the most courageous people I know, because they have been willing to pay the price to follow their convictions about the truth.

In spite of the challenges, many do leave Mormonism to seek a spiritual home in another church — for whatever reason. It is worthwhile to build relationships and make the effort to sustain spiritual conversations. Your LDS neighbor is a valuable person and is worth having as a friend, no matter how he or she responds when you share elements of your faith. God can use you to help your friend navigate the questions and doubts as they arise, and hopefully to discover the unconditional grace of God and the joy of eternal assurance.

WON'T YOU BE MY NEIGHBOR?

I N EACH CHAPTER we have introduced some ways that understanding our LDS neighbors might help you interact more wisely with them. I want to summarize and expand on those reflections.

While LDS life and culture are interesting, our purpose in studying Mormonism is not academic. I want you to understand your LDS neighbors so that you can be used by God to engage them redemptively as valuable persons loved by their Creator. Knowing about our neighbors helps us to build relationships with them, which in turn gives us the opportunity to share the good news of God's grace in a way that sounds like good news to them. As we prepare ourselves for spiritual conversations, we hope to see their spiritual thirst stirred rather than see them push up their walls of defense.

WE CAN DO BETTER

Historically, evangelical Christians have interacted with Mormonism in two ways. The first is mutual isolation. Mormons can get pretty wrapped up in their own all-encompassing world, with all their time and energy invested in their ward and family, which leaves little space for outside relationships. Traditional Christians have kept Latter-day Saints at arm's length because they seem different or because we have concerns about being targeted for conversion.

The second way evangelicals have related to the LDS community is by challenging their claims using traditional apologetics. Apologetics means "defense of the faith." A lot has been written to defend historic, biblical Christianity against the assertions of Mormonism. With three-fourths of LDS converts coming from traditional Christian churches, we need to teach the members of our churches how to evaluate Mormonism in light of the Bible.

Apologetics has also been used as the primary method of evangelizing Latter-day Saints. We have put a great deal of energy into challenging LDS doctrinal and historical claims, hoping that Latter-day Saints will be convinced that their beliefs are wrong and ours are right. This approach ignores the variety of reasons why people make faith commitments and fails to take into account that Latter-day Saints don't approach truth the same way evangelicals do. They don't make spiritual decisions on the basis of cognitive proofs. They have culturally ingrained prejudices against the methods we use. We do need to know the answers to LDS claims and be able to defend biblical truth.

EVANGELICAL "WITNESS" TO LATTER-DAY SAINTS HAS OFTEN CENTERED ON DISPROVING THE CLAIMS OF JOSEPH SMITH. © Utah State Historical Society, all rights reserved. Used by permission.

At some point in a relationship, an informed discussion of competing beliefs and truth claims must occur. Yet, we must also figure out how to present the good news of God's grace in ways that speak not only to a Mormon's mind but to the whole person in the context of their culture.

The apologetics approach is essentially negative. The message Latter-day Saints hear from us is not an invitation to embrace Jesus Christ in a new, liberating way. Rather, Mormons hear us tearing down their prophet and trying to destroy their church. Apologetics ministries focus more on proving Mormonism wrong than offering good news, as if the desired result is nothing more than for people to leave the LDS Church. I know a man who faithfully shared materials critical of Mormonism with an acquaintance. The information eventually got through and the man became convinced that Mormonism was wrong, angrily abandoning any prospect of faith in God. There was no relationship built and no good news offered. What good is it for a person to reject Mormonism but not come to trust in Jesus alone?

FIND COMMON GROUND

Building a relationship that leads to genuine engagement takes time and effort. You have to decide that it's worth the investment. Jesus said, "As the Father has sent me, I am sending you" (John 20:21). The Father sent Jesus to leave heaven and enter our world. He did not communicate with us from a distance or in some impersonal manner. In the same way, Jesus now sends us out of our comfortable world to enter our neighbors' world. It cost Jesus something to come and live among us, and it will cost us something to enter our neighbors' lives.

The first step is to find common ground. Active Latter-day Saints can be hard to get to know. Their relational needs are met through the ward, and they may have questions about your motives. There will be misunderstandings. Begin slowly. Start up a casual conversation in the yard or the break room. Don't begin with religion, but take an interest in all of life. Remember, not all Saints are the same. Ask questions and listen. You don't know what anyone believes or values until they tell you. One young LDS couple was struggling privately with doubts about Mormonism. They met a Christian neighbor at a block party. His kindness toward them helped make them receptive to another family's invitation to their church. They are now valued members of our congregation.

Serve your neighbor. Someone once said, "Love is the soil in which seeds of truth grow." We demonstrate our love and cultivate the soil of someone's heart by genuine acts of practical compassion. LDS people live busy lives. Offer to babysit or help with a yard project. It opens doors when you ask for their help. Welcomed invitations like these might give you an opportunity to invite them over for a cookout or to go to a movie or a ballgame — but not on Sunday! When we hosted a Christmas open house, our most active LDS neighbors came and stayed quite a while. We learned that the wife works in the same field as my wife and that we had several mutual acquaintances.

Jesus taught us that genuine love is unconditional. Value your LDS neighbors because they are persons whom God loves, regardless of whether they ever respond to your overtures. There is nothing wrong with being intentional about a relationship or with praying for God to use the relationship redemptively. God was intentional toward us, but he was also authentic. In my college days, I was pretty out of touch relationally. I once befriended a guy in my PE class just so I would have someone to bring to an outreach event. I wanted him to hear about Jesus, but I didn't really value him personally. He didn't go to the event; he could see right through my hypocrisy. I learned that if a relationship is only of value because of some desired result, it becomes manipulative.

The family is a good starting place when looking for ways to build common ground. Share about your family and ask about theirs. Offer to do something simple together as a family, like snacks or a game night. Talk about your parenting concerns and what you are learning as a parent.

If your neighbor asks you to read the Book of Mormon, consider it an opportunity to ask questions and share your input. In return, you may want to invite your neighbor to read the New Testament with you and talk about it. Don't let it degenerate into an argument. You don't have to defend your point of view. Just share your perspective about what you're reading and trust in the Holy Spirit's power at work through the Bible.

THINK CROSS-CULTURALLY

Our relationship with Latter-day Saints goes beyond merely what they believe. Remember what matters to them. They value the Church itself as the agency of God's work in this world. It makes sense that they react defensively when people speak ill of their Church. They love and value their prophets. It's easy to make cutting comments or jokes about the General Authorities. I've heard some wild accusations about LDS leaders. They value Joseph Smith. If his story is true, you can understand why. I believe there are many problems with Smith's credibility. Tread lightly when talking about him. Gauge the level of trust in the relationship before you speak. Latter-day Saints value their families. They value achievement. They value worthiness. Each of these values should give us some idea about where to start a conversation and what kind of things we should not say lightly.

Starting with the apostle Paul, Christians have always adapted their witness and lifestyle to reach people of different cultures. In Acts 13, Paul proclaimed the good news of Jesus to a Jewish group in Pisidian Antioch. In Acts 14, he preached to rural pagans in Lystra. His audience in Athens (Acts 17) was philosophically sophisticated urbanites. With each audience, Paul started with different assumptions and used a different method to explain the truth. There is only one message of salvation, but Paul adapted his approach in each different cultural setting.

Paul explained his strategy in 1 Corinthians 9:20–22. He said:

> To the Jews I became like a Jew, to win the Jews. To those under the law I became like one under the law (though I myself am not under the law), so as to win those under the law. To

those not having the law I became like one not having the law (though I am not free from God's law but am under Christ's law), so as to win those not having the law. To the weak I became weak, to win the weak. I have become all things to all people so that by all possible means I might save some.

The apostle consciously adapted himself to different audiences — without compromising fundamental principles — so that people would have an opportunity to be saved. We should adopt certain practices to relate to Mormonism. Our church operates a preschool because children are important to the Latter-day Saints and they have a lot of them. We should also avoid certain practices. For example, because many of my neighbors are LDS, I don't mow my lawn on Sundays. I don't drink alcohol, even though the Bible allows it. I have chosen to become like a Mormon to win the Mormons, by adapting in any way that I reasonably can.

STORIES AND EXPERIENCES

Mormonism is not primarily defined by theological statements of doctrine as much as it is by experiences and stories — like the stories of Restoration and eternal progression. We can learn how to frame our beliefs in story form rather than just a list of theological declarations. After all, the Bible communicates truth in the form of redemptive stories rather than concise statements of faith. The biblical story of God's redemption has four movements: God's good creation, humanity's fall into sin, God's saving work through Jesus, and the renewal of all things in the end. Think about how to share your own redemption story in light of God's great story, including your testimony of how you came to know Jesus, what your relationship with him is like, and what he has done in your life. It's easy to get into a debate about comparative beliefs, but it's hard to argue with or write off someone's story.

Experience is important to Latter-day Saints. In the past, this has made evangelicals uncomfortable, and we have often sought to minimize the emphasis on experience in order to shift the focus to doctrine. This is an overreaction. The faith we have to offer to Latter-day Saints is not limited to theological truth but entails a living relationship with God. We have our own encounters with the Spirit of God, both tender and powerful. Our witness will make more sense to Mormons if we embrace experience and learn to speak about it.

Speaking the language of experience means that we can talk about what God has done and is doing in our lives — not just our testimony of salvation, but stories of God's care, provision, answered prayer, and even discipline.

We need to express doctrinal truths in experiential language. I can debate with a Latter-day Saint all day long about whether God has a body or whether he is one being in three persons, and I won't get very far. But the truth might be heard in a new way if I talk about my experience with that truth. I might say:

I think the Trinity is the only way to describe God that is faithful to everything taught in the Bible, even though I can't fully understand how it works. When I consider how God is so much greater than anything my finite mind can comprehend, I want to kneel down in humility before him and worship him. I get overwhelmed with praise when I think of a God who is too great for my mind to grasp.

I believe that God is an immaterial spirit because that's how he reveals himself in the Bible. When the Bible talks about God's hands or face, it is speaking metaphorically, just like when it describes him as a consuming fire. That's the only way we can talk about God within our limited human frame of reference. What I find truly moving is the knowledge that God, as a Spirit, is not limited to one place at one time. Every day I count on knowing that whatever I'm facing, God is right there with me at the time. When I can't be with my children, I know that God is not just watching from afar but is with them, wherever they are. I can't tell you what a tremendous comfort the infinite presence of God is to me and my family.

PITFALLS TO AVOID

If you are willing to engage your LDS neighbor in spiritual conversations, you need to be prepared. Be ready to invest the time. Prepare yourself intellectually. Be able to answer the common LDS claims about apostasy, priesthood, continuing revelation, the Book of Mormon, and so on. Be prepared to explain key biblical doctrines like the Trinity, salvation by grace, heaven, the nature of sin, and the like. Latter-day Saints are well versed in the reasons for their faith, so you need to know the core issues as well.

You need to be prepared spiritually. Pray regularly for your friend. Recruit others to pray for you. Take a look at your life. Your words will have no credibility to Latter-day Saints if you aren't living in obedience to Jesus. That commitment needs to be visible in how you treat people and what you live for.

One common pitfall has to do with the meaning of words. Latter-day Saints use much of the same faith vocabulary as traditional Christians — words like "salvation," "born again," "the fall," "heaven," "eternal life," "faith," and "grace." These words have different meanings for our LDS neighbors than they have for us. Mormon doctrine can appear on the surface to be much more in line with historic biblical beliefs than it really is. Mormons may assume that we understand or agree with them because they are not aware of what we mean when we use certain words. The terminology creates confusion both ways, so we have to constantly define what we mean.

Latter-day Saints believe that contention is of the devil.[1] If we allow ourselves to fall into heated arguments, they will withdraw, and we will lose credibility.

Be sensitive about issues that offend Latter-day Saints. Saints are offended when their faith is misrepresented, as when someone says, "Mormons don't believe in Jesus," or when we equate them with the polygamist splinter groups. They are also offended when members of other churches deny that Mormons are Christians. (See Appendix B.)

The Latter-day Saints may be particularly thin-skinned about criticism because of past persecution and present-day prejudices. Avoid anything that seems mocking or disrespectful. Be truthful, but speak the truth with gentleness and respect. I don't believe that the LDS temple is sacred but because Latter-day Saints do, I will treat the subject respectfully. No matter how careful you are, you will probably offend your neighbor at some point simply by raising certain issues. Your friend may back away. Be patient and keep finding ways to serve and love your neighbor.

Latter-day Saints are offended by what they call "anti-Mormon literature" — anything written to attack or tear down the LDS Church.

CONSUMER PRODUCTS AND SOUVENIRS UNDERSCORE THE REVERENCE LATTER-DAY SAINTS FEEL TOWARD THEIR LEADERS. © Quinn Dombrowski. Used by permission via Creative Commons.

Since you know that they are trying to convert people out of existing churches, it is appropriate to evaluate and challenge their claims. Yet there is an element of truth in the LDS concern. Much that has been written over the years about Mormonism is caustic, argumentative, inaccurate in facts, and mocking in tone. Thankfully there are some responsible websites and resources that do a good job, more so now than ever before. (See Appendix C.)

Most Latter-day Saints fear the prospect of apostasy. All faiths have members who privately harbor doubts, but in the close-knit LDS society, where people speak publicly with so much certainty about their convictions, there are few avenues to express questions and concerns.[2] Asking too many questions openly leads to suspicion that apostasy may be taking root. It can be challenging for a Mormon even to admit questions or doubts to himself or herself because to break with Mormonism threatens one's entire identity, way of life, family relationships, and community standing. Be empathetic of this struggle. Many people are leaving Mormonism to follow Jesus in a whole new way, but it isn't easy.

WHAT WE HAVE TO OFFER TO LATTER-DAY SAINTS

Certain topics may be more fruitful than others for creating spiritual thirst in our LDS neighbors. Traditional Christianity has four blessings to offer to Latter-day Saints. First, we can offer fulfillment of the human desire for transcendence. We have a joy that comes from finding our proper place in the universe, as finite creatures of a magnificent, infinite God. Invite your friend to a worship service or Christian concert, where he or she can experience what it is like to enter the presence of the highest possible Being. Be careful about factors that might make a Latter-day Saint cringe. Make sure the venue is safe from toxic attitudes or references about Mormonism. Before you go, talk about some of the unfamiliar things they will encounter. Be willing to go to a Sacrament Meeting with your neighbor in return and discuss the two different experiences.

Second, we can offer our Mormon friends the delight of an intimate relationship with God. Even though Latter-day Saints see themselves as literal children of Heavenly Father, their relationship with God is more like servants than children. Servants do what they are supposed to do because they are bound by duty and obligation. Obedience results in a wage: a direct, measured reward. Children also obey, but they have a delight in their father that leads to an intimacy with him. It becomes a joy, not an obligation, to obey him. Unlike servants, children are not rewarded by a wage commensurate to their work but are smothered with generosity by their loving parents.

We can point our LDS neighbors toward a life with God that is energizing and alive, where we have direct access to our Father without a hierarchy of human authorities standing between. Hopefully you find it a joy, not a requirement, to read the scriptures and pray. I trust that you attend worship on Sunday not as a duty but as an opportunity to meet with God. If your relationship with God is based on obligation rather than delight, perhaps you should reevaluate some things before you talk to your Mormon neighbor.

A third fruitful area of discussion is our security before God. The Saints have a grand vision of what they might become in eternity, but they believe that no one can know in this life where they really stand with God or whether they have done enough to merit the celestial kingdom. In my last conversation with my LDS father before he passed away, he told me that his hope before God was that he had done his best. How can anyone be sure that they have always done their best? I know I haven't. We can bear witness of the assurance that comes not from our own efforts, but from the promises of God. We can be confident of our eternal destiny based on God's mercy, not our own merit.

The fourth blessing we have to offer Latter-day Saints is related: the good news of God's grace lavished on us in Jesus Christ. We can offer them hope when the pressure to perform becomes overwhelming, point them toward God's unconditional favor when they realize they can't be worthy enough, and invite them to receive God's free gift when they are crushed by trying to earn eternal rewards. We are both incredibly joyful and sobered knowing that when we can't measure up, Jesus has already done everything we need. It's ours simply by recognizing our spiritual poverty and trusting in him.

Of course, if we talk about grace, it requires that we practice unconditional grace in how we treat Latter-day Saints. The awareness of spiritual poverty will not come overnight. You may never see a hint of it at all. You need to persevere. Maybe a time will come when your friend's life collapses. Then you will be there, and everything you have shared and modeled about God's grace will kick in.

Former LDS President Gordon B. Hinckley said, "We say to people: you bring all the good that you have, and let us see if we can add to it."[3] We don't accept that premise. We believe that the Bible is sufficient. We believe that God has preserved his church on the earth since Jesus' day. We believe that what Jesus accomplished on the cross for us is enough. We find the biblical concept of heaven to be wonderfully satisfying. Mormonism has many strengths. We admire how Latter-day Saints live out their family life, their morality, their work ethic, and their care for each other. Mormons are great folks, but we believe they are incomplete without the gifts that historic, biblical Christianity has to offer them.

This is why we seek to understand our LDS neighbors and why we emphasize new ways of thinking about and interacting with them. They are valuable to God. The message of God's grace in Jesus Christ is good news for them. If we are willing to enter their world and learn of their ways, we can share this liberating message with this unique people.

SHOULD I VOTE FOR A MORMON?

WHEN MITT ROMNEY ran for President in 2008, many evangelical Christian leaders expressed concern about his Mormon faith. Twenty-nine percent of Republicans — presumably reflecting the conservative evangelical wing of the party — indicated that they probably or definitely would not vote for a Mormon for President. Yet many other Latter-day Saints serve in elected positions, both at a national and local level. Do traditional Christians have reasons for opposing a candidate who is Mormon?

Americans have elected presidents before with religious beliefs outside of biblical Christianity. Thomas Jefferson rejected the doctrines of the Trinity, original sin, and the atonement of Christ. Abraham Lincoln attended séances. As a Unitarian, William Taft rejected the deity of Christ. It seems that every viable candidate feels compelled to claim some form of Christian faith, but the public is content not to ask many questions about the nature or depth of a candidate's religious commitments, as long as that faith profession is generic or mainstream.

Mormons are treated differently. Some people cannot articulate reasons for opposing a Mormon candidate other than the simple fact of the candidate's religion. This strikes me as a form of bigotry.

Many of those averse to an LDS candidate have made their concerns clear. Fears exist that a Latter-day Saint in high public office would be more loyal to Mormonism than to the United States, giving undue influence to the wishes of the LDS Church. The heretical beliefs of Mormonism are a concern for others. Although the U.S. Constitution forbids a religious test for public office, it would be naïve to think that a candidate's deepest values and beliefs would be irrelevant to his or her fitness to govern.

Since Mormonism is a movement on the fringes of American normalcy, some object that a Latter-day Saint candidate could not truly represent a majority of Americans. The most common objection is that Mormonism gains legitimacy if LDS candidates are elected; that is true only if we assume that public exposure will advance the cause of the LDS Church and result in more people putting their eternal destiny in the hands of a false religion.

Each voter needs to evaluate the validity of those concerns. Conspiracy fears seem far-fetched. Latter-day Saints already hold positions of power, but there is no evidence that LDS apostles are pulling the strings behind the scenes. LDS lawmakers do not vote in unison or hold the same views on the issues. The highest ranking Mormon in public office, Senate Majority Leader Harry Reid, is a liberal Democrat. I'm not sure how a person's views on the Trinity have anything to do with his or her ability to govern well.

The discomfort among evangelicals with Mitt Romney in particular in the last election had less to do with his religious beliefs than with doubts about his credentials as a true social conservative. Personally, I am most troubled by the idea of Mormonism gaining converts through greater public exposure. But I'm not sure electing Mormons to high positions will cause that to happen. It seems that the Romney candidacy actually made the public more aware of the theological differences. Ironically, some Latter-day Saints worry that the increased exposure a high level candidate will bring to Mormonism will largely be negative.

In the end, evangelical Christians who support an LDS candidate do so for two reasons. First, they approve of the candidate's philosophy of government. Second, they agree with the particular policy positions that candidate supports. Voters will have to decide whether concerns over Mormonism outweigh the prospect of electing the men and women who might otherwise best represent their views.

ARE MORMONS CHRISTIANS?

WHEN LATTER-DAY SAINTS assert that they are Christians, many evangelicals disagree. Latter-day Saints, in turn, are confused and hurt by this denial. How do we handle it when our LDS neighbors ask, "Do you believe Mormons are Christians?"

I try to avoid discussing this issue when it's framed in this way. It doesn't usually lead anywhere fruitful because Mormons and evangelicals define "Christian" in completely different ways.

Latter-day Saints use a broad definition: a Christian is someone who follows Jesus Christ. They point out that Jesus is central to their Church's very name. Mormons believe that Jesus was born in Bethlehem, healed the sick, raised the dead, and offered himself as a sinless sacrifice for the sins of the world. They believe that he literally rose from the dead and lives today. They commemorate his death in every Sunday service and conclude their prayers in his name. So they are bewildered when anyone claims that they are not Christian.

Latter-day Saints also have in mind an ethical or behavioral definition: Christians are people who live Christlike lives. They point to their lifestyle, which embodies "Christian" virtues like marital fidelity, obedience to God, service, tithing, charitable action, and the like. When people claim Mormons aren't Christian, it comes across to Latter-day Saints as saying, "Your upright way of life is not recognized as valid."

Based on that broad definition, the LDS Church has a pretty good claim to make. Jesus Christ does have a central role in their beliefs and practices. Mormonism is certainly within the Christian family of religions compared to Buddhism, Islam, and Hinduism.

Latter-day Saints view themselves not only as legitimate Christians, but as the only fully authentic Christians. After all, the LDS Church claims to be the only valid representative of Jesus Christ on earth. It portrays itself as the complete restoration of what Jesus originally established. Joseph Smith said that God told him that all the churches were wrong, that their creeds were abominable to him, and that those who professed those creeds were all corrupt. Latter-day Saints may say they respect other churches and don't attack other people's faith, but Smith's claims can only be understood to mean that Mormons are the only fully authentic Christians and all others are Christian in some lesser sense or in name only.

As evangelicals, we use the word "Christian" in different ways among ourselves, depending on the context. We are willing to use "Christian" in a broad sense when we're talking about the whole historic Christian tradition. We talk about Nestorian Christianity or Catholic Christianity even though we disagree with the Nestorian view of the natures of Christ or the Catholic view of justification. We include the Episcopal Church in the Christian family even though we are concerned about their views on homosexuality. Many Mormons find this to be a confusing double standard. For evangelicals, "Christian" means something different when applied to an institution than it does when applied to an individual. We are asking, on one hand, is Mormonism Christian? And on the other hand, are Mormons Christians? In response to both questions, evangelicals use a narrow definition of the word.

When it comes to institutions — like a particular college, agency, or denomination — we typically use a theological definition. The institution in question is called "Christian" based on what it professes as truth, a shorthand designation for a particular set of beliefs. Mormonism is denied the title based on unbiblical beliefs and practices, such as deification of humans, God as an exalted man with a physical body, a second chance for salvation after death, and so forth. This narrower definition is an attempt to coalesce essential, biblically derived doctrines on key issues — such as God, humanity, creation, salvation — that have characterized Christianity worldwide since the first century. When we ask if an institution is Christian, we mean: Does it stand within the mainstream of historic, biblical Christian doctrine, by virtue of what it asserts to be ultimately true? From this perspective, some LDS doctrines are so far outside the historic Christian faith tradition that they mark Mormonism as essentially a foreign religion.

When it comes to individuals, we typically use an experiential definition. We call a person a "Christian" based on his or her status in relation to God. Is that individual regenerate and heaven-bound; is he or she under condemnation or under grace? We teach that this right standing with God is a function of a person's response of saving faith in God's gracious work. None of us can see a person's heart, so we have no absolute assurance of where anyone stands with God.

We typically use "Christian" to refer to individuals who confess that they are right with God by virtue of their trust in the saving work of Christ alone. Certain basic truths must be believed, but merely believing those truths does not constitute a person as a Christian in this sense. A changed lifestyle is expected as the consequence, and thus as some sort of evidence, of salvation. According to this experiential definition, we would certainly not assume that a person is a Christian simply because of the church he or she joins. One Baptist pastor in Utah sought to bring clarity to this by preaching a sermon series called, "Are Baptists Christian?" It was an effective way to illustrate that the issue goes far beyond mere labeling. In other words, when we ask if an individual is a Christian, we mean: Has that person trusted in God's provision through Jesus Christ so as to effect an eternal, spiritual change in his or her life?

To help a Latter-day Saint friend gain some empathy for why this is a troubling issue to evangelical Christians, you might consider an analogous situation within Mormonism. Polygamist groups in the news in recent years are offshoots of the LDS Church. They are referred to by themselves and others as "Fundamentalist Mormons." The LDS Church objects strenuously to anyone using the word "Mormon" in reference to these groups. They are basically trying to control who has the right to use the name "Mormon." The fundamentalists can make a valid claim on the name "Mormon" based on their loyalty to Joseph Smith and the Book of Mormon, but what the polygamists stand for is at odds with the mainstream LDS Church. They don't want polygamists identified with them by use of the same label. They have some values and boundaries they want to maintain. They want the world to think certain things when they see the word "Mormon."

In a similar way, evangelicals are uncomfortable about Latter-day Saints using the title "Christian." Mainstream Christians have some values and boundaries they want to uphold. Mormonism stands for some things that are at odds with historic Christianity. My point is simply that if Latter-day Saints don't want fundamentalist groups to be called "Mormon," they should at least have some empathy with why we are hesitant to apply the title "Christian" to them.

Why all the fuss over what seems to be a debate about labels and definitions? I believe evangelicals respond as they do because the LDS claim to be Christian glosses over fundamental differences between Mormons and traditional Christians. Educated people from both groups understand the differences, but the general populace, from which Mormonism draws its converts, probably does not. Evangelicals harbor some suspicion that the issue is driven by a desire to reduce negative perceptions so that more people will join the LDS Church. I don't know whether this suspicion is warranted, but it derives from the Church's practice of glossing over the core beliefs that distinguish Mormonism from historic Christianity and of refusing to reveal the "meat" of its teachings to investigators, which seems deceptive. Evangelicals respond strongly out of concern that the "Christian" label might attract unwitting converts to Mormonism from existing Christian churches.

Mormonism has to be considered "Christian" in the broadest sense of the word. Nobody owns the definition of the word, and Latter-day Saints are followers of Jesus Christ according to their understanding. Yet, Mormonism stands outside the stream of historic, biblical Christianity. Latter-day Saints would not deny this. In fact, they would not want to be considered Christian on these terms. When it comes to individual Mormons, no one can ultimately discern another person's interior condition. A Latter-day Saint may have a saving relationship with God as described above, but we can't assume so. The more closely someone adopts the Mormon worldview, the less likely he or she is to be right with God on those terms. This is why we must share the good news of God's grace through Jesus Christ with them.

In the end, this amounts to little more than a debate over labels. Without a common definition of "Christian," we end up talking past each other. We should be talking with our LDS friends about the fundamental issues behind the labels. What is the significance of Jesus' work on the cross? What is our eternal destiny? How does a person receive forgiveness of sins? When the question comes up, I try to redirect it to those more substantive topics.

RESOURCES FOR FURTHER STUDY

LDS SOURCES

The following sampling of sources describes Mormonism and Mormon culture from a loyal LDS perspective, including both official and unofficial viewpoints.

Publications

Contemporary Mormonism, by Claudia Bushman. Praeger Publishers, 2006.

The Encyclopedia of Mormonism. Not published by the LDS Church, but written by LDS scholars, this extensive resource is available at the Brigham Young University website: http://eom.byu.edu/index.php/Encyclopedia_of_Mormonism.

Gospel Principles. The official introduction to the basic teachings of Mormonism can be found at the LDS Church's official website: http://lds.org/gospellibrary/materials/gospel/Start%20Here_01.pdf.

Joseph Smith: Rough Stone Rolling, by Richard Bushman. Vantage Books, 2005.

Mormonism: A Very Short Introduction, by Richard Bushman. Oxford University Press, 2008.

Mormonism for Dummies, by Jana Riess and Christopher Bigelow. Wiley Publishing, 2005.

People of Paradox, by Terryl Givens. Oxford University Press, 2007.

Websites and Blogs

The Church of Jesus Christ of Latter-day Saints: www.lds.org

The LDS Church's official site for its members includes church magazines and curriculum manuals.

Meridian Magazine: www.meridianmagazine.com

By Common Consent: http://bycommonconsent.com
Mormon Matters: http://mormonmatters.org

SCHOLARLY / NEUTRAL SOURCES

Joseph Smith, Jesus, and Satanic Opposition, by Douglas J. Davies. Ashgate, 2010.

The Mormon Culture of Salvation, by Douglas J. Davies. Ashgate, 2000.

Mormon America, by Richard and Joan Ostling. HarperOne, 1999.

EVANGELICAL SOURCES

These sources, among others, offer good information about LDS truth claims, the differences between Mormon and Christian beliefs, and insights into how to share your faith with LDS friends and neighbors.

Publications

I Love Mormons, by David L. Rowe. Baker, 2008.

Mormonism Explained, by Andrew Jackson. Crossway, 2008.

The Mormon Mirage, by LaTayne Scott. Zondervan, 2009.

The Mormon Scrapbook, by Daniel G. Thompson. Providence Publications, 2004.

Speaking the Truth in Love to Mormons, by Mark Cares. WELS Outreach Resources, 1998.

Understanding the Book of Mormon, by Ross Anderson. Zondervan, 2009.

Websites and Blogs

Institute for Religious Research: www.irr.org
Mormon Coffee: http://blog.mrm.org/
Mormonism Research Ministry: www.mrm.org
The Religious Researcher: http://www.religiousresearcher.org/blog/
Utah Advance: www.utahadvance.org
Utah Lighthouse Ministry: www.utlm.org

NOTES

CHAPTER : PREFACE

1. John L. Sorenson, *Mormon Culture: Four Decades of Essays on Mormon Society and Personality* (Salt Lake City: New Sage, 1997), 27.

CHAPTER 1: MORMONISM: CULT OR CULTURE?

1. "2000s: The First Decade — Mormon Church Influence Soars," *The Deseret Morning News* (January 1, 2010).

2. David Van Biema, "The Church and Gay Marriage: Are Mormons Misunderstood?" *Time* (June 22, 2009). www.time.com/time/magazine/article/0,9171,1904146,00.html (accessed September 17, 2010).

3. "A Portrait of Mormons in the U.S," *The Pew Forum on Religion and Public Life*. http://pewforum.org/Christian/Mormon/A-Portrait-of-Mormons-in-the-US.aspx (accessed August 17, 2010).

4. Richard Lyman Bushman, *Mormonism: A Very Short Introduction* (New York: Oxford Univ. Press, 2008), 1 – 2.

5. Gary C. Lawrence, *How Americans View Mormonism: Seven Steps to Improve Our Image* (Orange, CA: Parameter Foundation, 2008), 17 – 18.

6. Ibid., 63 – 66.

7. Jessie L. Embry, *Mormon Wards as Community* (Binghamton, NY: Global Publications, 2001), 135.

8. Bushman, *Mormonism*, 102.

9. Spencer J. Palmer, "Comments on Common Ground," in *Mormons and Muslims: Spiritual Foundations and Modern Manifestations*, updated and revised ed.; ed. Spencer J. Palmer (Provo, UT: Religions Study Center, 2002), 88.

10. Douglas J. Davies, *The Mormon Culture of Salvation* (Burlington, VT: Ashgate, 2000), 6.

11. Sorenson, *Mormon Culture*, 140.

12. Ibid., 139.

13. Ibid., 140.

14. Davies, *The Mormon Culture of Salvation*, 137.

15. Howard R. Lamar, *The Theater in Mormon Life and Culture* (Logan, UT: Utah State Univ. Press, 1999), 5.

16. Michael Hicks, *Mormonism and Music: A History* (Urbana, IL: Univ. of Illinois Press, 1989, 2003).

17. Terryl L. Givens, *People of Paradox: A History of Mormon Culture* (New York: Oxford Univ. Press, 2007), 261.

18. Ibid., 268.

19. Katherine Ball Ross, ed., *The Mission: Inside the Church of Jesus Christ of Latter-day Saints* (New York: Warner, 1995), 20.

20. William A. Wilson, "The Study of Mormon Folklore: An Uncertain Mirror for Truth," in *The Marrow of Human Experience: Essays on Folklore*, ed. Jill Terry Rudy (Logan, UT: Utah State Univ. Press, 2006), 185 – 87.

21. Sorenson, *Mormon Culture*, 142.

22. Davies, *The Mormon Culture of Salvation*, 116.

23. Jana K. Riess, "Stripling

Warriors: The Cultural Engagements of Contemporary Mormon Kitsch," *Sunstone* 22, no. 2 (June 1999): 37.

24. Ibid., 45.

25. Jan Shipps, *Signifying Sainthood* (Logan, UT: Utah State Univ. Press, 2002), 8 – 29.

26. Bushman, *Mormonism*, 85.

27. Eric A. Eliason, "The Cultural Dynamics of Historical Self-Fashioning: Mormon Pioneer Nostalgia, American Culture, and the International Church," *Journal of Mormon History* 28, no. 2 (Fall 2002): 168 – 69.

28. Ross, *The Mission*, 99.

29. Mary Ellen Robertson, "Still Circling the Wagons: Violence and Mormon Self-Image," *Sunstone* 40, no. 4 (April 2002): 64 – 66.

30. Jan Shipps, "Making Saints: In the Early Days and the Latter Days," in *Contemporary Mormonism: Social Science Perspectives*, ed. Marie Cornwall, Tim B. Heaton, and Lawrence A. Young (Urbana and Chicago: Univ. of Illinois Press, 2001), 73.

31. Ibid., 74 – 77.

32. W. F. Walker Johanson, *What Is Mormonism All About?* (New York: St. Martin's Griffin, 2002), 201.

33. Ross, *The Mission*, 10, 12.

34. Clark L. Kidd and Kathryn H. Kidd, *A Convert's Guide to Mormon Life* (Salt Lake City: Bookcraft, 1998), 224 – 37.

35. Jana Riess and Christopher Kimball Bigelow, *Mormonism for Dummies* (Hoboken, NJ: Wiley, 2005), 85 – 88.

36. Rodney Stark, "The Rise of a New World Faith," in *Latter-day Saint Social Life: Social Research on the LDS Church and its Members*, ed. James T. Duke (Salt Lake City: Bookcraft, 1998), 14.

37. Shipps, "Making Saints," 78 – 79.

38. Sorenson, *Mormon Culture,* 9.

39. "A Portrait of Mormons in the U.S."

40. Sorenson, *Mormon Culture,*18.

41. Armand L. Mauss, "Mormonism in the New Century," *The Future of Mormonism*, at www.patheos.com/ Resources/Additional-Resources/ Mormonism-in-the-New-Century (accessed August 17, 2010).

42. William A. Wilson, "On Being Human: The Folklore of Mormon Missionaries," in *The Marrow of Human Experience: Essays on Folklore*, ed. Jill Terry Rudy (Logan, UT: Utah State University Press, 2006), 204 – 205.

43. *The Random House Dictionary of the English Language*, ed. Stuart Berg Flexner and Leonore Crary Hauck, 2nd ed., unabridged (New York: Random House, 1987).

CHAPTER 2: THE MORMON WORLDVIEW

1. Sorenson, *Mormon Culture,* 91.

2. Claudia L. Bushman, *Contemporary Mormonism: Latter-day Saints in Modern America* (Westport, CT: Praeger, 2006), 16. The closest thing to a definitive statement of faith in Mormonism is the Articles of Faith, a brief statement of certain tenets written down by Joseph Smith in response to an inquiry. It can be found in the LDS scripture called *The Pearl of Great Price* (Salt Lake City: The Church of Jesus Christ of Latter-day Saints, 1982), 60.

3. Davies, *The Mormon Culture of Salvation*, 196.

4. Givens, *People of Paradox*, 221.

5. Bushman, *Contemporary Mormonism*, 19.

6. Davies, *The Mormon Culture of Salvation*, 12 – 13.

7. Bushman, *Mormonism*, 5.

8. Ibid., 4.

9. Bushman, *Contemporary Mormonism*, 142.

10. Davies, *The Mormon Culture of Salvation*, 12.

11. Bushman, *Mormonism*, 71 – 74.

12. Ibid., 73.

13. Riess and Bigelow, *Mormonism for Dummies*, 23 – 27.

14. Elma W. Fugal, "Salvation of the Dead," in *Encyclopedia of Mormonism*, ed. Daniel H. Ludlow (New York: Macmillan, 1992), 1257 – 58.

15. Riess and Bigelow, *Mormonism for Dummies*, 35 – 39.

16. Van Biema, "The Church and Gay Marriage."

17. Bushman, *Contemporary Mormonism*, 23.

18. Richard Lyman Bushman, *Joseph Smith: Rough Stone Rolling* (New York: Vintage, 2007), 421 – 22.

19. Davies, *The Mormon Culture of Salvation*, 67.

20. Ross J. Anderson, "The Virtues of Hard Work and Self-Reliance Rooted in Biblical Versus Latter-day Saint Worldviews," *Trinity Journal* 27 n.s., no.1 (Spring 2006): 63 – 75.

21. Bushman, *Mormonism*, 74 – 78.

22. Massimo Introvigne, "Latter Day Revisited: Contemporary Mormon Millenarianism," in *Millennium, Messiahs, and Mayhem: Contemporary Apocalyptic Movements*, ed. Thomas Robbins and Susan J. Palmer (New York and London: Routledge, 1997), 238.

23. Armand L. Mauss, "The Fading of the Pharaohs' Curse: The Decline and Fall of the Priesthood Ban against Blacks in the Mormon Church," in *Neither White nor Black: Mormon Scholars Confront the Race Issue in a Universal Church,* ed. Lester E. Bush Jr. and Armand L. Mauss (Midvale, UT: Signature, 1984), 174 – 76.

24. On the use of the Bible in Mormonism, see Ross Anderson, *Understanding the Book of Mormon: A Quick Christian Guide to the Mormon Holy Book* (Grand Rapids: Zondervan, 2009), ch. 6.

25. For a brief introduction to the Book of Mormon, see ibid., chs. 1 and 2.

26. For a brief introduction to the other LDS scriptures, see ibid., ch. 5.

27. Blake Ostler, "The Challenges of (Non-existent?) Mormon Theology," *The Future of Mormonism*, at www.patheos. com/Resources/Additional-Resources/ The-Challenges-of-Non-existent- Mormon-Theology.html (accessed August 17, 2010).

28. Robert L. Millet and Gerald R. McDermott, *Claiming Christ: A Mormon-Evangelical Debate* (Grand Rapids: Brazos, 2007), 31 – 32.

29. Davies, *The Mormon Culture of Salvation*, 17.

CHAPTER 3: THE ONE TRUE CHURCH

1. Section 1:30 in The Doctrine and Covenants (Salt Lake City: Church of Jesus Christ of Latter-day Saints, 1982).

2. Davies, *The Mormon Culture of Salvation*, 176.

3. Johanson, *What Is Mormonism All About?* 210.

4. Bushman, *Mormonism*, 35.

5. Ross, *The Mission*, 78.

6. Davies, *The Mormon Culture of Salvation*, 24.

7. Spencer W. Kimball, "Remember the Mission of the Church," *Ensign* (May 1982), 4.

8. Peggy Fletcher Stack, "New LDS emphasis: care for the needy," *The Salt Lake Tribune* (December 10, 2009).

9. Ross, *The Mission*, 101.

10. This hymn can be found at http://library.lds.org/nxt/gateway.dll/Curriculum/music.htm/hymns.htm/restoration.htm/27%20praise%20to%20the%20man.htm#JD_Hymns.27 (accessed September 17, 2010).

11. Bushman, *Mormonism*, 51.

12. Bushman, *Contemporary Mormonism*, 39.

13. Alan K. Parrish, "Keys of the Priesthood," in *Encyclopedia of Mormonism*, ed. Daniel H. Ludlow (New York: Macmillan, 1992), 780–81.

14. Davies, *The Mormon Culture of Salvation*, 85–86.

15. Bushman, *Mormonism*, 50–51.

16. Ross, *The Mission*, 116.

17. Embry, *Mormon Wards*, 135; Bushman, *Mormonism*, 14.

18. Ross, *The Mission*, 139.

19. Ibid., 92.

20. Johanson, *What Is Mormonism All About?* 138.

21. Ibid., 138–39.

22. Riess and Bigelow, *Mormonism for Dummies*, 134.

23. Ibid., 138–39.

24. Bushman, *Contemporary Mormonism*, 33.

25. Bushman, *Mormonism*, 51–52.

26. Givens, *People of Paradox*, 10–15.

27. Ibid., 5–8.

28. Bushman, *Contemporary Mormonism*, 34.

29. Van Biema, "The Church and Gay Marriage."

30. Givens, *People of Paradox*, 16–19.

31. Ross, *The Mission*, 82.

32. Bushman, *Contemporary Mormonism*, 134.

33. Shipps, "Making Saints," 80.

34. Section 93:36 in *The Doctrine and Covenants*, quoted in Ross, *The Mission*, 54.

35. Stanley A. Peterson, "Institutes of Religion," in *Encyclopedia of Mormonism*, ed. Daniel H. Ludlow (New York: Macmillan, 1992), 684–685.

36. Givens, *People of Paradox*, 224.

37. Bushman, *Mormonism*, 40.

38. Bushman, *Contemporary Mormonism*, 136–37.

39. Jessie L. Embry, *Spiritualized Recreation: All Church Athletic Tournaments and Dance Festivals* (Provo, UT: Charles Redd Center for Western Studies, Brigham Young University, 2008), 37–47.

40. Ibid., 189.

41. Ibid., 184–85.

42. Kidd and Kidd, *A Convert's Guide to Mormon Life*, 227–228. Compare 1 Timothy 3:8–13.

CHAPTER 4: LIFE IN THE LOCAL CONGREGATION

1. Davies, *The Mormon Culture of Salvation*, 68.

2. Embry, *Mormon Wards*, 13–14.

3. Bushman, *Mormonism*, 106–7.

4. Embry, *Mormon Wards*, 23.

5. Ibid., 15.

6. Johanson, *What Is Mormonism All About?* 140.

7. Bushman, *Contemporary Mormonism*, 8.

8. Davies, *The Mormon Culture of Salvation*, 153.

9. Ross, *The Mission*, 49.

10. Givens, *People of Paradox*, 245.

11. Davies, *The Mormon Culture of Salvation*, 154.

12. Ross, *The Mission*, 136.

13. Embry, *Mormon Wards*, 14.

14. Davies, *The Mormon Culture of Salvation*, 200–201.

15. Ibid., 177.

16. William A. Wilson, "The Seriousness of Mormon Humor," in *The Marrow of Human Experience: Essays on Folklore,* ed. Jill Terry Rudy (Logan, UT: Utah State Univ. Press, 2006), 228.

17. Embry, *Mormon Wards*, 15.

18. Bushman, *Contemporary Mormonism*, 121.

19. Johanson, *What Is Mormonism All About?* 112.

20. Bushman, *Mormonism*, 55.

21. Johanson, *What Is Mormonism All About?* 95.

22. Ibid., 95.

23. Ross, *The Mission*, 46.

24. Ibid., 129.

25. "A Portrait of Mormons in the U.S."

26. Johanson, *What Is Mormonism All About?* 211.

27. Ross, *The Mission*, 120.

28. Bushman, *Contemporary Mormonism*, 8–9.

29. Johanson, *What Is Mormonism All About?* 200.

30. Ibid., 192.

31. Ibid., 193.

32. Ross, *The Mission*, 114.

33. Bushman, *Contemporary Mormonism*, 8–9.

34. Davies, *The Mormon Culture of Salvation*, 129–130.

35. Givens, *People of Paradox*, 48.

36. Rodney Stark, "The Basis of Mormon Success: A Theoretical Approach," in *Latter-day Saint Social Life: Social Research on the LDS Church and its Members*, ed. James T. Duke (Salt Lake City: Bookcraft, 1998), 63.

37. Johanson, *What Is Mormonism All About?* 86.

38. Ross, *The Mission*, 26.

39. Embry, *Mormon Wards*, 135.

CHAPTER 5: FAMILIES ARE FOREVER

1. Ross, *The Mission*, 7.

2. Bushman, *Contemporary Mormonism*, 82.

3. Brent Corcoran, ed., *Multiply and Replenish: Mormon Essays on Sex and Family* (Salt Lake City: Signature Books, 1994), vii.

4. Givens, *People of Paradox*, 39.

5. Davies, *The Mormon Culture of Salvation*, 143–45.

6. Ross, *The Mission*, 72.

7. Tim B. Heaton, Kristen L. Goodman, and Thomas B. Holman, "In Search of a Peculiar People: Are Mormon Families Really Different?" in *Contemporary Mormonism: Social Science Perspectives,* ed. Marie Cornwall, Tim B. Heaton, and Lawrence A. Young (Urbana and Chicago: Univ. of Illinois Press, 1994), 88–89.

8. Davies, *The Mormon Culture of Salvation*, 155.

9. "A Portrait of Mormons in the U.S.," see ch. 1, fn. 3.

10. Bushman, *Contemporary Mormonism*, 59.

11. Tim B. Heaton, "Vital Statistics," in *Latter-day Saint Social Life: Social Research on the LDS Church and its Members*, ed. James T. Duke (Salt Lake City: Bookcraft, 1998), 114.

12. Carrie A. Miles, "LDS Family Ideals versus the Equality of Women: Navigating the Changes since 1957," in *Revisiting Thomas F. O'Dea's The Mormons: Contemporary Perspectives*, ed. Cardell K. Jacobsen, John P. Hoffmann, and Tim B. Heaton (Salt Lake City: Univ. of Utah Press, 2008), 128.

13. Heaton, Tim B., "Four C's of the Mormon Family: Chastity, Conjugality, Children, and Chauvinism," in *The Religion and Family Connection: Social Science Perspectives*, ed. D. Thomas (Provo, UT: Religious Studies Center, Brigham Young University, 1988), 112.

14. Neylan McBaine, "The Future of Mormon Motherhood," *The Future of Mormonism*, at www.patheos.com/Resources/Additional-Resources/The-Future-of-Mormon-Motherhood.html (accessed August 17, 2010).

15. Bushman, *Mormonism*, 94.

16. Miles, "LDS Family Ideals," 129.

17. Bushman, *Contemporary Mormonism*, 41.

18. Ibid., 129.

19. Bushman, *Mormonism*, 110.

20. D. Michael Quinn, "Exploring Utah's Theocracy Since 1975: Mormon Organizational Behavior and America's Culture Wars," in *God and Country: Politics in Utah*, ed. Jeffery E. Sells (Salt Lake City: Signature, 2005), 140–44.

21. Jan Shipps, "The Persistent Pattern of Establishment in Mormon Land," in *God and Country: Politics in Utah*, ed. Jeffery E. Sells (Salt Lake City: Signature, 2005), 74.

22. Roger M. Thompson, *The Mormon Church* (New York: Hippocrene, 1993), 197.

23. Riess, "Stripling Warriors," 45–46.

24. Thompson, *The Mormon Church*, 195.

25. Bushman, *Contemporary Mormonism*, 44.

26. Ross, *The Mission*, 34.

27. This authoritative declaration describes both LDS family values and the worldview underlying them. It can be found at http://lds.org/library/display/0,4945,161–1–11–1,00.html (accessed September 16, 2010).

28. Riess, "Stripling Warriors," 46.

29. Danel W. Bachman and Ronald K. Esplin, "Plural Marriage," in *Encyclopedia of Mormonism*, ed. Daniel H. Ludlow (New York: Macmillan, 1992), 1091–95.

30. Bushman, *Mormonism*, 91.

31. Bushman, *Contemporary Mormonism*, 51.

32. Hunter's relationship with the two wives is described in "Sister Hunter's Humor and Cheerfulness Remembered as She Is Laid to Rest," *Deseret News* (October 22, 2007).

CHAPTER 6: SACRED SPACE

1. Bushman, *Contemporary Mormonism*, 78.

2. Temple statistics come from www.ldschurchtemples.com/statistics/ (accessed September 6, 2010).

3. Johanson, *What Is Mormonism All About?* 133.

4. Ross, *The Mission*, 140.

5. Davies, *The Mormon Culture of Salvation*, 72 – 79.

6. Bushman, *Mormonism*, 57 – 58.

7. Davies, *The Mormon Culture of Salvation*, 82.

8. Loren Marks and Brent D. Beal, "Preserving Peculiarity as a People: Mormon Distinctness in Lived Values and Internal Structure," in *Revisiting Thomas F. O'Dea's* The Mormons: *Contemporary Perspectives*, ed. Cardell K. Jacobsen, John P. Hoffmann, and Tim B. Heaton (Salt Lake City: Univ. of Utah Press, 2008), 279.

9. Davies, *The Mormon Culture of Salvation*, 4.

10. Bushman, *Contemporary Mormonism*, 80.

11. Bushman, *Mormonism*, 57.

12. Johanson, *What Is Mormonism All About?* 205.

13. Davies, *The Mormon Culture of Salvation*, 74.

14. Ibid., 83.

15. Ross, *The Mission*, 145.

16. Bushman, *Mormonism*, 62.

17. Ibid., 61.

18. Bushman, *Contemporary Mormonism*, 85.

CHAPTER 7: LATTER-DAY SAINT PIETY

1. Ross, *The Mission*, 78.

2. Givens, *People of Paradox*, 26.

3. Bushman, *Mormonism*, 28 – 29.

4. William A. Wilson, "Teach Me All That I Must Do: The Practice of Mormon Religion," in *The Marrow of Human Experience: Essays on Folklore,* ed. Jill Terry Rudy (Logan, UT: Utah State Univ. Press, 2006), 255.

5. Stark, "The Basis of Mormon Success," 58.

6. Section 93:36 in *The Doctrine and Covenants.*

7. Noel B. Reynolds, "Brigham Young University: A Special Commitment to Faith," in *Mormons and Muslims: Spiritual Foundations and Modern Manifestations*, ed. Spence J. Palmer, updated and revised edition (Provo, UT: Religions Study Center, 2002), 47. Quoting Doctrine and Covenants 88:118 and 88:79.

8. Givens, *People of Paradox*, 238.

9. Riess, "Stripling Warriors," 44.

10. Calvin L. Rampton, "Toleration of Religious Sentiment," in *God and Country: Politics in Utah*, ed. Jeffery E. Sells (Salt Lake City: Signature, 2005), 87.

11. Bushman, *Contemporary Mormonism*, 22.

12. "All is Safely Gathered In: Family Home Storage," www.providentliving.org/fhs/pdf/WE_FamilyResourcesGuide_International_04008_000.pdf (accessed September 9, 2010).

13. Davies, *The Mormon Culture of Salvation*, 219.

14. Gordon B. Hinckley, "Personal Worthiness to Exercise the Priesthood," *Ensign* (May 2002).

15. Alma 7:15 in *Book of Mormon* (Salt Lake City: Corporation of the President of The Church of Jesus Christ of Latter-day Saints, 1981). Cited in an LDS teacher's manual for Primary 3:

Choose the Right B; http://lds.org/
ldsorg/v/index.jsp?hideNav=1&locale=0
&sourceId=47560f9856c20110VgnVCM1
00000176f620a_____&vgnextoid=637e1b
08f338c010VgnVCM1000004d82620a
RCRD (accessed September 8, 2010).

16. Davies, *The Mormon Culture of Salvation*, 162.

17. "Standards Summary," *For the Strength of Youth*; http://lds.org/library/display/0,4945,30 – 1 – 7 – 9,00.html. (accessed September 7, 2010).

18. Bushman, *Mormonism*, 39.

19. Marks and Beal, "Preserving Peculiarity as a People," 260 – 64.

20. Romel W. Mackelprang, " 'They Shall Be One Flesh': Sexuality and Contemporary Mormonism," in *Multiply and Replenish: Mormon Essays on Sex and Family*, ed. Brent Corcoran (Salt Lake City: Signature, 1994), 48.

21. Johanson, *What Is Mormonism All About?* 116.

22. Marks and Beal, "Preserving Peculiarity as a People," 263.

23. Peggy Fletcher Stack, "Spiritual confections," *The Salt Lake Tribune* (September 17, 2005).

24. Bushman, *Contemporary Mormonism*, 49.

25. "A Portrait of Mormons in the U.S."

26. Johanson, *What Is Mormonism All About?* 189 – 90.

27. Ross, *The Mission*, 17.

28. Johanson, *What Is Mormonism All About?* 100.

29. Ibid., 197.

30. Armand L. Mauss, "Feelings, Faith, and Folkways: A Personal Essay on Mormon Popular Culture," in *'Proving Contraries': A Collection of Writings in Honor of Eugene England*, ed. Robert A. Rees (Salt Lake City: Signature, 2005), 25 – 28.

31. Davies, *The Mormon Culture of Salvation*, 175.

32. Bushman, *Contemporary Mormonism*, 17.

33. Givens, *People of Paradox*, 32. For an example, see Stephen E. Robinson, "Believing Christ," *Ensign* (April 1992), 5, for the story of Janet Robinson.

34. Latter-day Saints point out the flaws in using negative statistics about Utah as a whole to draw conclusions about Mormonism, but many LDS writers are happy to assume that positive statistics about Utah are due to the LDS majority.

35. Rebecca Walsh, "Statistics paint ugly postcard," *The Salt Lake Tribune* (March 16, 2008).

36. Givens, *People of Paradox*, 276.

37. For example, see Millet and McDermott, *Claiming Christ*, 183 – 88.

CHAPTER 8: US AND THEM

1. Bushman, *Contemporary Mormonism*, 135.

2. Sorenson, *Mormon Culture*, 145.

3. Givens, *People of Paradox*, 27 – 28.

4. Wilson, "The Seriousness of Mormon Humor," 226 – 27.

5. Bushman, *Mormonism*, 103 – 4.

6. Armand L. Mauss, *The Angel and the Beehive: The Mormon Struggle with Assimilation* (Urbana: Univ. of Illinois Press, 1993), 197 – 198.

7. Riess, "Stripling Warriors," 46.

8. Stark, "The Basis of Mormon Success," 47 – 49.

9. Armand L. Mauss, "Mormonism in the New Century."

10. Noah Feldman, "What Is It about Mormonism?" *The New York Times* (January 6, 2008). For an example of this phenomenon, see David van Biema, "Kingdom Come," *Time* (August 4, 1997): 56. In this article Gorden B. Hinckley professed ignorance about whether God was once a man.

11. Jerry Johnston, "Milk before Meat," *The Deseret News* (July 18, 2010).

12. Bushman, *Contemporary Mormonism*, 133.

13. Sean P. Means, "Hey, guys, mormons are cool!" *The Salt Lake Tribune* (August 10, 2010).

14. Missionary statistics come from the official media information site for the LDS Church: http://lds.org/ldsnewsroom/eng/statistical-information (accessed September 9, 2010).

15. Tally S. Payne, "'Our Wise and Prudent Women': Twentieth Century Trends in Female Missionary Service," in *New Scholarship on Latter-day Saint Women in the Twentieth Century*, ed. Carol Cornwall Madsen and Cherry B. Silver (Provo, UT: Joseph Fielding Smith Institute for LDS History, Brigham Young University, 2005), 133.

16. Bushman, *Contemporary Mormonism*, 59 – 61.

17. Bushman, *Mormonism*, 46 – 47.

18. Stark, "The Basis of Mormon Success," 57 – 58.

19. Ibid., 56 – 57.

20. Joseph Smith, 2:19 in *The Pearl of Great Price* (Salt Lake City: The Church of Jesus Christ of Latter-day Saints, 1982).

21. Davies, *The Mormon Culture of Salvation*, 223.

22. Bushman, *Mormonism*, 60.

23. Givens, *People of Paradox*, 58.

24. Bushman, *Mormonism*, 40.

25. Shipps, "The Persistent Pattern of Establishment in Mormon Land," 68.

26. "Articles of Faith," in *The Pearl of Great Price*, 60.

27. "A Portrait of Mormons in the U.S."

28. Rampton, "Toleration of Religious Sentiment," 87 – 90.

29. Peggy Fletcher Stack, "Have LDS, Jews resolved proxy baptism dispute?" *The Salt Lake Tribune* (September 9, 2010).

30. Stephen Stromberg, "What Matters about Romney," *The Washington Post* (February 17, 2007).

31. "Mormons feel the backlash over their support of Prop. 8," *The Los Angeles Times* (November 19, 2008).

32. Jan Shipps, "Romney campaign was a mixed blessing for Mormons," *The Salt Lake Tribune* (February 9, 2008).

33. See "Preach My Gospel," ch. 3, at http://lds.org/library/display/0,4945,8057 – 1 – 4424 – 1,00.html (accessed September 9, 2010).

CHAPTER 9: JOINING AND LEAVING

1. Growth statistics come from the official media information site for the LDS Church: http://lds.org/ldsnewsroom/eng/statistical-information (accessed September 11, 2010).

2. "A Portrait of Mormons in the U.S."

3. David G. Stewart Jr., "The Future of Mormon Missionary Work," *The Future of Mormonism*, at www.patheos.com/Resources/Additional-Resources/Future-of-Mormon-Missionary-Work.html (accessed August 17, 2010).

4. David Stewart, *LDS Church Growth, Member Activity, and Convert Retention: Review and Analysis,* www.cumorah.com/index.php?target=church_growth_articles&story_id=8 (accessed September 11, 2010).

5. O. Kendall White Jr., "Thomas F. O'Dea and Mormon Intellectual Life: A Reassessment Fifty Years Later," in *Revisiting Thomas F. O'Dea's* The Mormons: *Contemporary Perspectives,* ed. Cardell K. Jacobsen, John P. Hoffmann, and Tim B. Heaton (Salt Lake City: The Univ. of Utah Press, 2008), 30–33.

6. Stan L. Albrecht, "The Consequential Dimension of Mormon Religiosity," in *Latter-day Saint Social Life: Social Research on the LDS Church and its Members,* ed. James T. Duke (Salt Lake City: Bookcraft, 1998), 253–292.

7. Mark J. Cares, *Speaking the Truth in Love to Mormons* (Milwaukee: WELS Outreach Resources, 1998), 158–16.

8. Bushman, *Mormonism,* 114–16.

9. Shipps, "Making Saints," 80.

10. Stewart, *LDS Church Growth, Member Activity, and Convert Retention.*

11. "A Portrait of Mormons in the U.S."

12. Stan L. Albrecht and Howard M. Bahr, "Patterns of Religious Disaffiliation: A Study of Lifelong Mormons, Mormon Converts & Former Mormons," *Journal of Scientific Study of Religion* 22, no. 4 (December 1983): 366–79.

13. Todd Compton, "Apostasy," in *Encyclopedia of Mormonism,* ed. Daniel H. Ludlow (New York: Macmillan, 1992), 56.

14. "Be Not Deceived, but Continue in Steadfastness," *Doctrine and Covenants and Church History Gospel Doctrine Teacher's Manual* (Salt Lake City: The Church of Jesus Christ of Latter-day Saints, 1999), 134.

15. Section 10:27–33 in *The Doctrine and Covenants* and 3 Nephi 26:4 in *Book of Mormon.*

16. Stan L. Albrecht and Howard M. Bahr, "Strangers Once More: Patterns of Disaffiliation from Mormonism," *Journal of Scientific Study of Religion* 28, no. 2 (June 1989): 180–200.

17. D. Jeff Burton, "The Phenomenon of the Closet Doubter," in *The Wilderness of Faith: Essays on Contemporary Mormon Thought,* ed. John Sillito (Salt Lake City: Signature, 1991), 82.

18. Bushman, *Contemporary Mormonism,* 135.

19. William Lobdell, "Losing faith and lots more," *The Los Angeles Times* (December 1, 2001).

20. Burton, "The Phenomenon of the Closet Doubter," 83.

21. Ibid., 82.

22. On New Order Mormons, see http://www.newordermormon.org/ (accessed September 11, 2010).

23. Burton, "The Phenomenon of the Closet Doubter," 83–84.

CHAPTER 10: WON'T YOU BE MY NEIGHBOR?

1. 3 Nephi 11:2–30 in *Book of Mormon.*

2. Givens, *People of Paradox,* 32.

3. "Gordon Hinckley: Distinguished Religious Leader of the Mormons," *Larry King Live* (September 8, 1998), available at www.lds-mormon.com/lkl_00.shtml (accessed September 12, 2010).

DISCUSSION GUIDE

CHAPTER 1: MORMONISM: CULT OR CULTURE?

1. In what ways have you encountered Mormons or Mormonism?
2. What elements define a culture? Do you agree or disagree that Mormonism constitutes a unique culture? Why?
3. What formative experiences have shaped your identity? How do those compare with the influences that shape the LDS identity?
4. Thinking about Latter-day Saints whom you know, in what ways are they different from each other? What features do they share in common?
5. What comes to your mind when you think of the word "cult"? In what ways is it accurate or inaccurate to think of Mormonism as a cult?
6. In what ways does it help or hinder our witness to Latter-day Saints to refer to Mormonism as a cult?

CHAPTER 2: THE MORMON WORLDVIEW

1. What is a "worldview"? What are some key elements of your worldview?
2. In what ways do Latter-day Saints think about or formulate truth differently from traditional Christians?
3. What stories from your heritage help shape how you think and what you value?
4. What impact might the story of the Restoration have on how Latter-day Saints view themselves and others?
5. Summarize the Mormon story of salvation. How is it different at key points — creation, God, humanity, eternity, etc. — from the historic Christian story?

6. What are the sources traditional Christians look to as authoritative? What sources in our world are analogous to LDS leaders and "folk Mormonism"?

CHAPTER 3: THE ONE TRUE CHURCH

1. What does the author mean when he says, "The LDS Church is the matrix in which salvation is achieved"?
2. In what ways do traditional Christians approach the whole issue of "church" differently from Latter-day Saints?
3. What factors make you feel positive about the church you attend? What are some reasons why Latter-day Saints revere their Church so much?
4. What is your relationship with the denomination or movement that your congregation is part of? How does that compare to Latter-day Saints' relationship with the LDS Church?
5. Summarize the LDS Church's governing hierarchy. Compare this to the organizational structure of your denomination or association.
6. How is the New Testament idea of priesthood similar to or different from the LDS priesthood?

CHAPTER 4: LIFE IN THE LOCAL CONGREGATION

1. Explain the relationship between the LDS Church and its local wards.
2. What are the pros and cons of organizing congregations geographically, with set boundaries? Of sharing a building between different congregations? Of scheduling all church meetings in one block?
3. How is a Mormon bishop similar to and different from a Christian pastor or priest?

4. What would you be interested in looking for or finding out if you attended an LDS Sacrament Meeting? (Perhaps your group can arrange to attend a Sacrament Meeting together sometime soon.)
5. What are some factors at your congregation that you would have to be careful about or explain in advance if your neighbor was going to visit your worship service?
6. How open do you feel about developing a deeper friendship with a Latter-day Saint? Why do you feel that way?

CHAPTER 5: FAMILIES ARE FOREVER

1. What are some of the LDS family values that you also appreciate or share? What are some of their family values that you can't relate to? Why?
2. What is the underlying view of families in Mormonism that drives their values?
3. What does the author mean when he says, "The eternal family lineage stretches backward as well as forward"?
4. What are some ways that Latter-day Saints reinforce the importance of family in their daily lives?
5. What are some specific ways that the topic of "family" can open the door to build common ground with Latter-day Saints?
6. What will it cost us to build relationships with our Mormon neighbors? How do you feel about paying that price?

CHAPTER 6: SACRED SPACE

1. How are the physical and social environments of the temple and the ward different?
2. Why are temples so valued by Latter-day Saints? What are some important ideas and values that get reinforced in the temple experience?

3. What do you think about the idea of performing ordinances by proxy for those who have died? How does this practice fit in to the overall LDS worldview?

4. How and why do you suppose the temple experience creates "a church within a church"?

5. Why are Latter-day Saints reluctant to talk about their temple experiences?

6. How will Mormons react when things associated with the temple are treated lightly by outsiders? What issues might make you feel the same way?

CHAPTER 7: LATTER-DAY SAINT PIETY

1. How would you describe your spiritual conversion? How is that different from how Latter-day Saints view conversion?

2. In what ways are the ideals of "progress" and "worthiness" lived out by Latter-day Saints? How have you seen this with Mormons whom you know?

3. What are the drawbacks of placing so much emphasis on achievement and worthiness?

4. How are LDS spiritual practices similar to or different from your own?

5. What is the role of spiritual experiences in your Christian life? How does this differ from Mormonism?

6. How have you experienced the grace of God in a way that would be an encouragement to Latter-day Saints?

CHAPTER 8: US AND THEM

1. In what ways does Mormonism foster an "us versus them" mentality? Are there ways in which your church does so?

2. In what ways do you observe Mormonism moving toward assimilation with American culture? In what ways do you see it moving toward antagonism?

3. Give some examples you have seen of LDS public relations at work.

4. What is your impression of the life of a Mormon missionary? If the missionaries came to your door, how could you serve them?

5. What reasons do Latter-day Saints have to be sensitive about criticism or opposition? As a group, how are they perceived by the public compared to other cultural groups in America?

6. Would you read the Book of Mormon if asked? Would you take the missionary lessons? Why or why not? How far should we go in order to share our faith with our LDS neighbors?

CHAPTER 9: JOINING AND LEAVING

1. Why do people join the LDS Church? How does that compare to the reasons why you affiliated with the church you attend?

2. Why do people leave Mormonism?

3. Why, for many people, is it so difficult to leave Mormonism?

4. Why do you think the prospect of apostasy is so threatening to Latter-day Saints?

5. Why do people stay in Mormonism even when they no longer believe it?

6. How can you create the level of trust that it would take for a Mormon to confide in you with his or her doubts? What factors would build trust? What factors would destroy trust?

CHAPTER 10: WON'T YOU BE MY NEIGHBOR?

1. What are the strengths and weaknesses of traditional Christian apologetics when applied to Mormonism?

2. What are some ways to build common ground in any relationship? Specifically, with Latter-day Saints?

3. What does it mean to "think cross-culturally" toward Mormons?

4. The author gives two examples of how to express doctrinal truth in the language of personal experience. Can you think of others?

5. What are some pitfalls to avoid in sharing your faith with Latter-day Saints?

6. The author describes four elements of a positive witness toward Latter-day Saints. Can you think of other key ideas that might help create spiritual thirst in the hearts of people from Mormon culture?

APPENDIX A: SHOULD I VOTE FOR A MORMON?

1. People give various reasons not to vote for a Mormon candidate. Which reasons do you consider valid? Less than valid?

2. Are there other churches or religions whose members you would hesitate to vote for? What are they? In each case, what makes you hesitant?

3. What are the reasons you usually vote for a candidate?

4. Are the issues the same for a candidate running for a local versus a national office? For a higher versus a lower office?

5. In what ways have your ideas on the subject changed since reading this appendix?

APPENDIX B: ARE MORMONS CHRISTIANS?

1. The author claims that the discussion of "Are Mormons Christians?" is not fruitful and should be avoided. Why does he say that? Do you agree or disagree? In what ways could this discussion be made fruitful?

2. In what ways do Mormons define who is or is not a Christian?

3. In what ways do evangelicals define who is or is not a Christian?

4. Do you accept the idea that we must use different definitions for institutions versus individuals? Why or why not?

5. The author says that "Mormonism has to be considered 'Christian' in the broadest sense of the word." Do you agree or disagree? Why?

6. Do you think it is possible for a person to be genuinely saved while being a member of the LDS Church? Why or why not?

Understanding the Book of Mormon

A Quick Christian Guide to the Mormon Holy Book

Ross Anderson

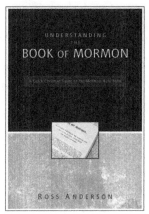

Mormons, or members of the Church of Jesus Christ of Latter-day Saints, form a growing population in both numbers and in influence. Yet few people have more than a passing knowledge of the document that defines and drives this important movement—the Book of Mormon.

A former Mormon and an adult convert to Christianity, author Ross Anderson provides a clear summary of the Book of Mormon including its history, teachings, and unique features. Stories from the author and other ex-Mormons illustrate the use of Mormon scripture in the Latter-day Saint church. Anderson gives special attention to how the Book of Mormon relates to Christian beliefs about God, Jesus, and the Bible.

With discussion questions to facilitate group use and a focus on providing an accurate portrayal of Mormons beliefs, *Understanding the Book of Mormon* is an indispensable guide for anyone wishing to become more familiar with the Church of Jesus Christ of Latter-day Saints and its most formative scripture.

Learn more at www.UtahAdvance.org

Available in stores and online!

Share Your Thoughts

With the Author: Your comments will be forwarded to
the author when you send them to *zauthor@zondervan.com*.

With Zondervan: Submit your review of this book
by writing to *zreview@zondervan.com*.

Free Online Resources at
www.zondervan.com

Zondervan AuthorTracker: Be notified whenever your favorite
authors publish new books, go on tour, or post an update
about what's happening in their lives at www.zondervan.com/
authortracker.

Daily Bible Verses and Devotions: Enrich your life with daily
Bible verses or devotions that help you start every morning
focused on God. Visit www.zondervan.com/newsletters.

Free Email Publications: Sign up for newsletters on Christian
living, academic resources, church ministry, fiction, children's
resources, and more. Visit www.zondervan.com/newsletters.

Zondervan Bible Search: Find and compare Bible passages in
a variety of translations at www.zondervanbiblesearch.com.

Other Benefits: Register to receive online benefits like
coupons and special offers, or to participate in research.

ZONDERVAN.com/
AUTHORTRACKER
follow your favorite authors